Rental Property Investing for Beginners

Build Your Long-Term, Multi-Million Dollar Empire
Through Multifamily, Airbnb, Commercial and Apartment
Building Real Estate

DAVID HARRIS

TABLE OF CONTENTS

INTRODUCTION

Are you looking for an investment that is better than the stock market? Or one where you can have more and better control over your investment returns and management?

There are many ways to generate wealth in real estate investing, but consider rental investing if you want the most lucrative of all. Rental investing offers the following investment returns:

- Cash flow

- Appreciation

- Depreciation

- Leverage

- Tax Benefits

In addition to your residential home, owning a rental property can be a way for you to generate income and build wealth.

In the United States alone, more than a third of US households dwell in rental housing. Following the Great Recession and housing market crash was the spike in the number of house renters across all households ethnicities/race. Significant increases were apparent, especially among higher-income and older households. However, households from younger members, low-income, and minority households still rent and make up a large part of the renters' population.

Although demands for rental homes are currently slowing down, demographic changes will continue to drive increases in the number of renter households in the coming years or even decades. Nevertheless, there seems to be a sweeping change in rental demands. Families that can afford to buy homes shifted their preferences to renting houses instead of buying.

According to America's Rental Housing Report published by the Joint Center for Housing Studies of Harvard University, there is a remarkable uptrend in rents. Most of the growth in renters is high across the country. High-income households have driven most of the growth in renters since 2010 (Joint Center for Housing Studies of Harvard University, 2017a).

About 30 percent of the growth of renters is driven by high-income households since 2010, and renting remains the primary option for those with less income. The majority of households (53%) earning less than $53,000 are living in rental homes, including households earning less than

$15,000 a month (60%)(Joint Center for Housing Studies of Harvard University, 2017b).

Buying other real estate properties aside from your home can generate wealth for you if investing in the stock market is not your choice.

Forty-seven percent of rental properties are owned by individual workers, according to data released in 2017 (Kolomatsky, 2017).

When investing in real estate, the goal is to put your money at work today to increase in time for you to have more money in the future. The return on your investment must be enough to cover the risk you are taking, the cost of owning the real estate property, including regular repair, maintenance, utilities, insurance, and taxes.

There are hundreds of ways to generate income through real estate, but the amount of time it takes to grow your real estate depends mainly on your investing strategy, skills, knowledge, and timeline.

For beginners in real estate investing, the concept can be as simple as playing the Monopoly game.

Once you learn the fundamental factors of economics, investment, and risk, the rest will be easy enough to put you on the trail of success. To win, you purchase properties, avoid getting bankrupt, and generate money through rentals so you can buy more properties to fill in your investment portfolio.

Nonetheless, you also have to keep in mind that "simple" does not necessarily mean easy, and committing a mistake can earn you consequences, which can range from minor inconveniences to major disaster.

THE BENEFITS OF RENTAL PROPERTY INVESTING

Rental property is a good way of securing an additional income stream. However, like any other investments, there are pros and cons that you need to know before getting into it. Once you are aware of them, you can analyze if this option is suitable for your situation and long-term financial goal.

Rental properties fall under the category of **income properties** which are properties bought and developed to earn revenue from them either through monthly cash flow or asset appreciation once you decided to sell them for a profit.

There are many benefits to buying an income property and have it rented. Here are some of them.

RENTAL INCOME BENEFITS

The most immediate benefit you can get from rental property investment is the income you derive from tenants. Ideally, it must offset the mortgage and managing cost incurred while having the property for rent. If the property sustains a positive rental yield, you later used the annual cash flow to develop the property, purchase additional property, or diversify your investment portfolio.

DIRECT CONTROL

When investing in rental property, you have direct control over your business like:

- Choosing what property to invest in

- Which type of tenants you'll cater to

- How much will be your monthly charge

- How you will manage and manage your property

- What conditions will you make for your lease contract

- Are you hiring a property management company/manager to help you find and service long-term renters

- Are you providing short-term vacation stays?

While investing in stocks and bonds gives you some freedom to choose your stocks and bonds to invest in, you still don't have complete control over your money.

PROPERTY APPRECIATION

Owning a rental property means that you can later benefit from the asset once it grows its property value. External variables, such as nationwide economy, population growth, and neighbourhood development, are the primary driver of property appreciation,

Although meaningful property value increases are not often certain, you can increase your chance to benefit from this by researching the location area before buying the property. By learning about the area's historic pricing data and projected development trends, you will determine if the property has potential value growth.

LEVERAGING CAPABILITY

One unique opportunity in real estate is to purchase a property using a small amount from your pocket and borrow the rest. We call this leveraging. If you bought a property using debt that is significantly bigger than the equity, then the investment is considered to be highly leveraged.

TAX INCENTIVE BENEFITS

There are several tax concessions you can claim if you are managing and maintaining a rental property.

If you have it on a mortgage, you can claim for annual loan interest and any origination fees as tax-deductible expenses.

As long as you can justify your relation to managing a rental property, you can apply deductions of the following expenses, including tax-deductible components.

- Property condition depreciation

- Maintenance and repair works

- Travel expenses

- Legal and management fees

The Internal Revenue Services will allow you to deduct expenses connected with the rental property under the categories of:

- Ordinary and necessary expenses

- Improvements

- Depreciation

RISKS ASSOCIATED WITH REAL ESTATE INVESTING

When it comes to real estate, rental properties are one of the most popular choices often picked by investors.

Investing in rental property has some definite drawbacks. Here are some of them.

- Cash flow

- Solid investment portfolio

- Diversified investments

- Rental property appreciation

In other words, investing in rental property is the best move you can do if you want to see and control your earnings directly over time.

However, you have to keep in mind that rental properties are not risk-free despite being the least risky of all options in real estate investing. Here is a list of the most significant risks associated with rental property investing:

BAD OR RUDE TENANTS

A landlord wants his property occupied whenever an opportunity comes. Nonetheless, there are times when the increase in occupancy may not be worth it. Before renting out the property, you must ensure that the tenants who will occupy your property will not cause headaches or financial losses. Therefore, screening tenants before considering handing them the key is necessary. Also, some tenants do not have impressive credit histories, which is not helpful to your business.

Although you may want to choose good tenants, you can never get away with bad ones. Some tenants could be delinquent in their payments, destructive, demanding, or neglectful in turning off the water, etc. Therefore, it is best to include occupancy or house rules, policies, and guidelines for tenants before accepting them. Also, requiring a security deposit proves to be helpful for get-away and destructive tenants.

Contacting their previous landlords to get some feedback on the tenant can be helpful. There's a chance that the tenant may have a habit of damaging someone's property, which can incur losses on your part.

BAD LOCATION

When it comes to investing in real estate, location is crucial. Whether you're planning to buy a rental property or any other type of real estate property, it is critical to consider the site itself. Some locations may seem like an ideal choice due to their low maintenance costs and higher occupancy rates.

However, this likewise indicates that the area not suitable for someone to live in because it is either underdeveloped or has a high crime rate.

It might be tempting to buy a rental property in a neighbourhood with a high crime rate since the prices are somewhat low. Nonetheless, owning a property in that kind of neighbourhood can put your property at risk. There is always a chance of it being vandalized. Any damage done to your property can result in unexpected expenses, including repairs and legal complications.

Conversely, buying a property in a bad neighbourhood that is showing signs of development in terms of improved law enforcement in the area might be worth the risk.

NEGATIVE CASH FLOW

The purpose of owning a rental property is to have a stable cash flow, which is the profit you earn from your property after lessening the taxes, expenses, and mortgage payment.

In other words, you have a positive cash flow if you can still earn some money after deducting those expenses, while a negative cash flow means that you have a deficit instead of earnings.

Factors such as rental property expenses, maintenance, mortgage, and low rent could trigger negative cash flow, so make sure to calculate everything before purchasing that property. Your calculation must include estimating both expected and unexpected expenses regarding your property that could potentially impact the entire outcome. Record even the smallest of expenses since it could become bigger soon.

MARKET ECONOMY PLUNGE

As a landlord, make sure that you are in touch with what's happening in the market economy, and you need to educate yourself to understand it. There are times wherein you may have been earning a positive cash flow on the property but, when the time comes when you're planning to sell it, the property's value has gone down considerably, resulting in it getting sold at a lower price. Because of this, it is a good idea to understand the market economy for you to be able to forecast whether it is a good time for selling properties or not.

HIGH VACANCY RATE

The most common and the most considerable risk that most rental property landlords often face is the risk of having high vacancy rates. Your greatest challenge is bringing in tenants to your property.

In a typical situation, you may want your vacancy rate to be below 10% or less to achieve maximum returns, though having at least 70-80% occupancy rate isn't a bad thing either. Additionally, money lenders and banks also take occupancy into account when it comes to lending landlords money. Most of them only lend to those with rental properties having over 70% occupancy rate or more.

Try calculating the expected vacancy rate of your rental property. It will prepare you to handle your finances properly even when a financial disaster strikes.

Even though rental properties are excellent forms of investment as they can generate passive income, it doesn't mean that they are easy to manage. Just looking at the risks mentioned above can make you think twice as an investor. So before trying to take the plunge, make sure that you have enough courage to see things through until the end.

LACK OF LIQUIDITY

Like all investments in real properties, rental property investing is one of the most illiquid assets. The liquidity of an asset refers to its ability to change into cash. Even the hottest property in the market takes several months to complete a sale. If you are selling your property because you need money for an emergency need, you will not get the best price.

For an average investor, acquiring a rental property, whether upfront or through a mortgage, can be a significant concentration of assets. Because real estate property is an illiquid asset, it is constantly exposed to risk in terms of property value and local demand for tenants.

RISING TAXES AND INSURANCE PREMIUMS

Although interests on mortgage and principals are fixed, taxes and insurance can increase more quickly than you can increase your rent.

ACTIVE MANAGEMENT

Owning a rental property is claiming an active role in its management, including:

- Screening and identifying reliable tenants

- Collecting monthly payments

- Maintaining the property's good condition at all times

- Ordering repairs

- Conducting regular house inspections

These are just some of your responsibilities as a rental property owner.

However, if you don't have the time or are not interested in taking this part, you may hire a management company to do all these tasks.

FACTORS TO CONSIDER IN RENTAL PROPERTY INVESTING

Pre-planning and homework are both required before investing in rental property to ensure its success. Consider the following elements listed below before deciding to become a landlord:

LOCATION

The rental property's location plays a significant role in this investment strategy since it directly affects the tenants, who can rent the property. It is ideal to buy property in places where you can comfortably deal with the general population living in the area. The location also affects the value of the property as well as its appreciation potential. In other words, properties located in depressed or dangerous regions will not have the long-term market value appreciation compared to those found inside peaceful and better neighbourhoods.

PRICE AND FINANCING

It is necessary to know the actual fair market price of an investment property to prevent paying for overpriced properties. You can find reasonable market prices for investment properties from a Comparative Market Analysis (CMA). You can determine a property's market value through the capitalization rate method. You can do this by taking the property's net operating income (NOI) and dividing it by its market value. The result, expressed in percentage, should be equal or greater than the similar investment properties in the area to ensure that you can profit from it.

When you acquire rental properties, make sure to examine the financing costs and methods adopted thoroughly before making an offer on the property. Getting pre-approved for mortgages is also recommended to gain credibility, leverage, and clout with the seller.

PROPERTY'S CONDITION

A low-priced bargain investment property or a 'fixer-upper' may look good at first glance. However, it can be an expensive money pit when it comes to expenses involving repairs and upgrades. Neglected properties in poor condition tend to have 'hidden defects' that you must address before applying the desired upgrades. Consider the renovation cost and the lost rent opportunity cost since it takes time to finish repairs and upgrades. So instead of buying a fixer-upper property, buying a more expensive but reliable 'turnkey' property is better when it comes to being cost-effective.

PROPERTY'S RENTAL INCOME

Some unethical sellers would 'inflate' the property's price by increasing rent. Sending estoppel emails to tenants who are currently occupying the property may help you verify actual rents.

On the other hand, the tenants will have to respond by confirming the actual rent they pay their landlord and conditions regarding their rental or lease agreements. It could also include the amount of security deposit that needs to be paid upfront upon sale of the property.

RENTAL PROPERTY MANAGEMENT

Whether you decide to do this personally or not, rental properties do need managers to stay operational. You either need to manage the property as the landlord or hire someone to do the managing work, which also means another set of expenses.

Factors that could affect your decision include:

- Rental property size

- Availability

- Management knowledge/skills

- Temperament for the job

If you find that managing work is not your thing, make sure to hire a reliable manager or avail services offered by a property management firm. Property management firms nowadays collect a part of the tenants' rent as their management fee. Nevertheless, keep in mind that there are also unethical property management firms, ones whom you should avoid at all costs.

ASSESSMENT METHODS

Many investors are becoming dissatisfied with the meagre returns they get from their savings and investments that they take a closer look at investing in rental property. Several years of recorded low-interest rates drive them away from investing in bonds, and they resort to commodities like real estate, which is perceived to be inflation-protected. The majority of investors want to diversify their investments which means they don't have to invest solely in equities or stocks.

All these give you the reason to get into rental property investing. However, before you do, you need to learn how to assess a property to determine if it is a good investment.

Here are two factors to help you in your property assessment.

THE CAP RATE

The cap rate is the profit you can generate from the revenues derived from the property or the Rate of Return you would make on a house if you bought it in cash. The formula for the cap rate is:

$$\textbf{Cap Rate} = \text{Net Income} / \text{Asset Cost}$$

For example, you buy a house worth $250,000 and have it fixed and rented for $2,000 per month.

You spent an average of $800 every month for repairs and

Your monthly expenses are $800, excluding the principal and interest payments on a mortgage. However, it includes the escrowed sum for insurance and taxes.

Your Net Operating Income on your rental property would be $ 1200 a month or an annual income of $14,400.

Now, we compute the cap rate

Cap rate: $14,400 / $250,000 = 0.06\%$

This cap rate can either be good or bad, depending on how you analyze the situation. If these come from quality tenants in a good neighbourhood, this cap rate could be a great return on your asset. Nevertheless, if the property happens to be in a shaky neighbourhood, which entails many risks, this 6% return on your investment might still be good enough.

THE ONE-PERCENT RULE

Generally, when assessing a rental property, people often use this rule of thumb. If the monthly rental income before expenses (gross income) equals at least one percent of the purchase price, they can consider the property for investment.

For example, you are considering buying a house for $250,000. In this case, you have to make sure that you can have it rented for at least $2,000 per month based on this rule of thumb. If it doesn't, then it is not feasible.

With 1% monthly, you will be earning annual gross revenue of 12% or a 68% net income every year. However, remind yourself that 6-8% of non-compounded interest does not mean anything. So if you want to give your investment the same benefit that money in the stock market can provide, reinvest 100 percent of your income back to allow it to accumulate compound by itself.

TYPES OF RENTAL PROPERTIES FOR INVESTMENT

There are many ways of utilizing rental properties to create income streams. Here are three ways to leverage rental properties for investment.

- Long-term rentals

- Short-term rentals

- Turnkey rentals

Short-term rentals are property investments designed for a few months or even weeks at a time. Purchasing a home or property located in a popular vacation spot will allow you to rent it out to tourists on vacation. Today, we also have this Airbnb trend among backpackers and tourists looking for a place to stay for a day or more. You may also purchase a condominium unit in a busy urban area and rent it out to business travellers in the short term.

Long-term rentals, on the other hand, are what people always consider when renting out their properties. These are properties rented out for one year or more. Examples of this property type are:

- Single-family homes

- Townhomes

- Duplex homes

- Condominiums

- Apartments

Turnkey rentals are similar to long-term rentals. They are also designed to be rented for extended periods. The only difference is that turnkey properties have everything in place to generate rental income. So when you purchase a turnkey rental, it already has rental property for renters in place and a property manager to oversee monthly collection and maintenance.

HOW RENTAL PROPERTIES CAN HELP YOU RETIRE EARLY THAN STOCKS?

Many investors are genuinely impressed with their investment returns on rental properties. Nevertheless, how can we compare rental property investment with the stock market?

You may want to invest in a rental property for diversification, but the first thing you must consider when starting to invest in something you had not tried before is the return on your investment. So, which asset class produced better returns in the long run? Is it real estate or stocks?

There is no definite answer to this question, but it may help you gain insights into how these two assets are comparable to each other as long-term investments.

It is essential to know that stocks generally increase in value faster than real estate. However, it is fair to say that real estate investments have more return potentials than stock investments. When combining price rental income potential, price appreciation, and inherent tax incentives of real estate investing, there is great potential for long-term returns on your investment.

So if you are trying to pursue early retirement or financial independence, you may as well learn the 4% Rule – assuming a 4% withdrawal rate when calculating to know if your investment portfolio will cover your cost of living. The Four Percent Rule is a rule of thumb used by many investors and financial analysts to determine how much a retiree should get out of their retirement account each year.

CHAPTER 1: GETTING INTO THE GAME WITH THE RIGHT MINDSET

W e often hear investors telling us that it takes knowledge, the right motivation, and strong determination to build a passive income stream via rental properties. However, we failed to realize how crucial it is to have the right mindset to succeed in any real estate venture.

Starting each day with a positive mindset is the most important step of your journey to discovering opportunity.

Jay Samit

When setting up goals – financial or otherwise – always start with the right mindset. Your mindset will help you get through during tough times, so you don't easily give up. The same thing works with rental property investing. Even when you are armed with perfect information, having learned everything you need to know to ready you before diving into investing, if your mind is afraid to take the risk, then you are bound to lose even with your 401k mutual funds.

Most often, we underestimate rental properties because they are not easy to analyze. With stocks, you have to know if they are going down or up and if you have tiny dividends on the side, you add that to the calculation.

However, with rental property, different components contribute to your return.

- Appreciation

- Cash flow

- Tax benefits

- Tenants who would be paying down the mortgage

- Inflation that would be eating bit by bit your mortgage

Investors in stocks would only focus on appreciation and cash flow, but in rental property investing, all these factors are mixed to make you a real winner.

Let's start having the right mindset.

The leveraging factor in rental property investing can scare away some would-be investors. Leveraging for them equates to DEBT, which can be scary. However, not all debts are bad. If you think debt is wrong, you use debt to buy an asset that is depreciating and isn't earning you any income.

An example of bad debt is when you buy a car through a financing company. Because the vehicle will not be helping you earn some money can pay for it, you will later find yourself buried in debt when you have no other source of income.

But if you buy a rental property on a mortgage, you will be paying for the mortgage using income earned from the rental. This way, the property itself is paying for your mortgage, which is good debt.

Leveraging is a powerful tool when it comes to rental properties. If you take advantage of the mortgage industry, you can start investing in real estate.

If you intend to get into rental property investing, you need to have a positive mindset. Remember that only a positive mindset can give you the right motivation and strong determination to start something.

IS REAL INVESTING FOR ME?

Real estate has become a playground for many of the world's most successful investors, so there are plenty of reasons to believe that it is a sound investment. However, not all are cut to be a landlord. Many have tried investments, and many likewise failed. Therefore, it's better to be well-informed before spending hundreds of dollars.

ARE YOU CUT TO BE A LANDLORD?

Are you a handyman?

How are you at handling your toolbox and doing some house repairs and maintenance tasks? Of course, you can always hire someone to these tasks for you or even have a property manager think of everything related to your business, but surely that would eat a large part of your income. Usually, property owners who have more than one home do their repairs. It saves them enough money for other expenses they could not do on their own.

If you are the handyman type and don't have much spare cash, property rental investing may not be suitable for you.

PAYING OFF PERSONAL DEBT

Seasoned investors have debts as part of their investment strategy. However, if you still have lots of obligations to pay off, like medical bills, student loans, or children who will be attending college soon, purchasing a rental property at this time may not be the right time for you to invest. Never put yourself in a position where your debt is more than what you can afford to pay. You can't use your income to pay down personal debts as you have to learn to separate personal from business.

SECURE A DOWN PAYMENT

Properties for investment generally require significant equity or down payment and have stricter requirements than properties that owners will occupy. You need at least 20% of the property cost for the down payment.

FINDING THE RIGHT LOCATION

You would not want to be stuck with a property in an area that is declining instead of one with high development potentials. A city or countryside area with a growing population and an ongoing development plan is a great investment opportunity to consider.

So when choosing a profitable rental property, find a location with low property taxes, plenty of amenities – like movie theatres, malls, parks, restaurants, access to public transportation, low crime rate, and a growing job market. This kind of setting could mean a large pool of tenants that is suitable for rental property investment.

Should You Pay in Cash?

You have two options when acquiring the property and it depends on your investing goals. When you choose to pay in cash, it can help you generate positive monthly cash flow. Let's say you acquire $100,000 worth of rental property. With the monthly income, deprecation, and all taxes, including income tax, you can get a 9.5 annual return or $9,500 in annual earnings.

However, financing can provide you with an even much greater return. So if you spend a 20% down payment on a house with a compounding mortgage of 4%, you can have around $5,580 annual income after deducting operating expenses and additional interest. You may see that the cash flow is lower than when you pay in cash, but a yearly return of 27.9% on your $20,000 investment is still much higher in profitability than a 9.5% return for a 100,000 investment.

AVOID HIGH -RATES

If you decide to finance your purchase, you will need a low-mortgage payment scheme to eat your monthly profit.

CALCULATE YOUR MARGINS

Set a goal of 10% return. Estimate annual maintenance costs at 1% of the property, and other expenses include

- Property taxes

- Homeowner's insurance

- Homeowner's association fees

- Monthly expenses

- Pest control

- Landscaping

- Additional maintenance and repair expenses

- Invest in Landlord Insurance

Consider having landlord insurance in addition to your homeowner's insurance. Landlord insurance generally covers lost rental income, property damage, and liability protection for a tenant or a visitor who may suffer an injury caused by property maintenance issues.

UNEXPECTED COST

Aside from upkeep and maintenance costs that will be eating up a part of your rental income, unexpected events may happen, like a damaged roof cause b a hurricane or burst pipes that will damage some parts of the house structure. To be ready for such emergency cases, plan to set aside 20-30% of your rental income for timely repairs.

AVOID A FIXER-UPPER

Who wouldn't want to get a house at a bargain and then flip it into a rental property? However, it would not be a good idea unless you are skilled at large-scale improvement to avoid paying too much for renovation. Instead, find a property with a price below the market and needs only minor repair works.

EVALUATE OPERATING EXPENSES

Initial operating expenses on a new property are generally between 35-80% of the gross operating income. Let's say you charge $1,500 for rent, and your monthly expenses are $600. Then your operating expenses are about 40%. For easy calculation, use the 50% rule, allocating half of your monthly rental income to expenses. So if your monthly payment is $2,000, definitely allocate $1,000 for expenses.

KNOW YOUR RETURN

Businesses are all about figures, and for every dollar, you invest, expect a good return for it. If you get a 6% return in your first year as a property investor, consider it healthy and anticipate it to rise every year or over time.

BUY A LOW-COST HOME

For an expensive home, expect a more significant expense required to maintain it. Expert investors recommend starting with a property that wouldn't cost you more than $150,000 in a good neighbourhood. Furthermore, they never buy the nicest or the worst house on the block.

BE AWARE OF LEGAL OBLIGATIONS

Before diving into the rental business, know your legal obligations as a landlord. You must be familiar with local and state landlord-tenant laws to avoid legal issues or deal appropriately with them. Have a clear understanding of your tenant's rights and your obligations regarding eviction rules, fair housing practices, lease requirements, etc.

AVOID A FIXER-UPPER

Who wouldn't want to get a house at a bargain and then flip it into a rental property? However, it would not be a good idea unless you are skilled at large-scale improvement to avoid paying too much for renovation. Instead, find a property with a price below the market and needs only minor repair works.

EVALUATE OPERATING EXPENSES

Initial operating expenses on a new property are generally between 35-80% of the gross operating income. Let's say you charge $1,500 for rent, and your monthly expenses are $600. Then your operating expenses are about 40%. For easy calculation, use the 50% rule, allocating half of your monthly rental income to expenses. So if your monthly payment is $2,000, definitely allocate $1,000 for expenses.

KNOW YOUR RETURN

Businesses are all about figures, and for every dollar, you invest, expect a good return for it. If you get a 6% return in your first year as a property investor, consider it healthy and anticipate it to rise every year or over time.

BUY A LOW-COST HOME

For an expensive home, expect a more significant expense required to maintain it. Expert investors recommend starting with a property that wouldn't cost you more than $150,000 in a good neighbourhood. Furthermore, they never buy the nicest or the worst house on the block.

BE AWARE OF LEGAL OBLIGATIONS

Before diving into the rental business, know your legal obligations as a landlord. You must be familiar with local and state landlord-tenant laws to avoid legal issues or deal appropriately with them. Have a clear understanding of your tenant's rights and your obligations regarding eviction rules, fair housing practices, lease requirements, etc.

WEIGH REWARDS VS. RISKS

In making your financial decisions, make sure that the payoff is worth the potential risks involved.

Rewards

- If real estate value increases, so will the value of your property investment.

- Once your investment is getting more stable, it can become more passive. Notwithstanding the upkeep cost and initial investment, you can still earn income while working on a regular job.

- The interest you are paying on your property loan is deductible from your income tax

- Despite economic crises, compared to other investment assets, real estate is generally more stable

- It is a tangible asset that can't be lost or stolen from you.

Risks

- If your property is vacant, you had to shoulder all the monthly expenses.

- Real estate is not a liquid which means, you can't easily convert it to cash. You first had to sell the property if you want its value in money.

- Your rental may not be enough to cover your mortgage payment.

- Although rental income is considered passive, tenants can be a pain in the neck.

When investing, you need to be realistic in your expectation. Like other investments, your rental property won't generate a significant monthly rental income right away. And picking up the wrong choice could be a catastrophe n itself for an investor.

So, for your first deal, consider working with an experienced partner or rent out your own home for a period to test if rental investing is right for you.

WHY MANY PROPERTY OWNERS FAIL?

Real Estate is a good investment, which was already tried and tested by many investors for decades. However, around half of them sell up after five years and those who managed to stay never bought a second property.

There are many reasons behind these things, but the reasons mentioned below are the most common.

LACK OR NO INVESTMENT EDUCATION

Most newbie investors are poorly educated about making a good investment that it is becoming a reason behind most failures committed in real estate investing. On the other side, knowledgeable investors, if not experts, succeed since they know how to distinguish between investment stocks and investment-grade properties. At the same time, they never cease studying their trade, making them more knowledgeable and competent as time goes.

NO DEFINITE REAL ESTATE INVESTMENT STRATEGY

Some real estate property owners fail, mainly because they have no solid strategy in the first place. They are the ones who just happened to have some money in their coffers and, after hearing something like, "Real Estate is a good source of passive income," they immediately rush in and join the bandwagon. Because of this, they give up after realizing that they made a wrong move either by purchasing the wrong house or accepting the bad tenants that will occupy their property. And since they chose to focus on cash flow rather than capital growth, most of them try it for a short while and then eventually give up in the end.

WRONG FINANCES

Most investors, especially new ones, don't have the necessary finance-related knowledge that will enable them to persevere in the long run. Rather than having a concrete financial strategy, they tend to overcommit financially, meaning that they just put in as much money as possible, thinking that they will have significant returns. They also choose and make loans based on the cheapest fees, or lowest interest rates provided instead of consulting a financial strategist that thinks a few steps ahead of them.

Savvy investors make a financial buffer through an offset credit line or account accessible whenever the investor faces a financial problem. They also tend to have the discipline to keep the 'rainy day' money and use it during a financial drought. They not only know how to buy properties; they can also buy time through their financial buffers.

SET AND FORGET

There is a relatively common mistake in real estate investing, known as the **Set and Forget** strategy. This good-sounding strategy promises investors with 'set and forget properties, which are said to be the kind that you'll just set up or modify one time and then forget since it will just grow in value over time. On the other hand, an intelligent investor knows that such a belief is rubbish since properties are prone to decay if left alone for a long time. They know that, once it shows pieces of wear, it won't attract tenants no matter how cheap the rent becomes. That's the reason why they regularly review their portfolio's performance to understand the ones that need necessary attention.

BAD MARKET TIMING

Some investors think of buying properties through the so-called 'market timing' strategy, which involves buying property in a particular location just because of an infrastructure project that will probably cause the area to prosper over time. Another trick involving this strategy is buying properties on the bottom tier of the market and then attempting to sell them at the highest possible price. Because of this, they end up buying property in a location that is not even performing on average, eventually causing financial loss rather than profit.

On the other hand, Savvy investors buy their next property whenever their finances allow them to rather than believe in market timing. They also tend to buy property in a location that they would be more than happy and willing to hold even for an extended period.

THE SWEET BENEFITS OF LEVERAGE

One benefit of investing in real estate is leverage. Leverage is using borrowed capital to increase potentials for profit in your investment. Using the power of leveraging is using other people's money so you can earn more money, especially when there is a spike in the value of properties. There are several ways you can get funding for an investment property.

GETTING ACCESS TO FINANCING

With good credit standing, it will be easy for you to acquire financing for a rental property.

Generally, a financing company will be charging an interest rate – usually 0.75-1.25%, which is much higher than loan assistance provided for primary residences. In addition, it also expects you to provide 20-30% equity. Banks and financing corporations consider an investment loan riskier than a home mortgage loan for a primary residence.

As we talk about mortgages, we can discuss the power of leveraging, which sets apart real estate investing from other investments. As we say, leveraging is about using other people's money to bring you income.

When you invest in the stock market, you are using your own money to control 100 percent of your investments. But in real estate, you only use 20-30% of your money to control the whole property. Hence, when generating monthly income out of that property or when you sell it, you are gaining revenue on the total value of your investment while multiplying your returns.

HOW LEVERAGE WORKS?

To be more precise in understanding what leverage in real property is, let us consider the following examples.

Example # 1

Joe bought an investment property worth $150,000 in spot cash and had it rented for $1,500 per month, bringing him gross annual revenue of $18,000. Assuming 35% ($6,300) of this gross income is spent for operating expenses, the average annual net income will be $11,700. The annual return is 7.8%.

Example #2

John bought five investment properties at $150,000 but only paid $30,000 each (20% of the individual property value for equity or down payment). Seventy percent of the total value of each of these properties was mortgaged. If he had his properties rented at $1,500 a month and 60% was spent for expenses including mortgage and taxes, each property will provide John with a net annual income of $7,200 each. Therefore his return on investment is 12 percent, which will earn John a yearly average profit of:

Annual Gross Income/Property

= $1,500 x 12 months = **$18,000**

Estimated Expenses (60% of Annual Gross Income)

= $18,000 x .60

= **$10,800**

Annual Net Profit Per Property

= Annual Gross – Expenses

= 18,000 – 10,800 = **$ 7,200 per property**

Total Annual Net Profit = $7,200 x 5 properties = **$36,000**

Return on Investment/Property

= Annual Net Profit/Equity = #7200/$30,000

= 24% or ROI on Total Investment =
$36,000/$150,000 =24%

In our example #2, John achieved 24% return on his investment of $150,000 compared to a return of 7.8 % for the same amount. Aside from a bigger return on his investment, which he will use to pay down his mortgage, he will have five properties in his name and a diversified portfolio.

Not only is John making more money than Joe, but he is also controlling $750,000 worth of real estate compare to Joe's $150,000 property. It could lead John to more opportunities for home value appreciation and lower risk because John has superior diversification.

The more properties you own, the more diversified your investment is and the more potential returns.

With five rental homes like John, you have better opportunities for better returns. Even when one property becomes unoccupied, the other four will provide you with an income buffer until you find a tenant for occupying it.

Another way to diversify your portfolio is to pick different locations or neighbourhoods, sizes, types, and classes of renters.

Because you can leverage your investment, you have to always think of it as a long-term investment.

WHEN IS LEVERAGE TOO MUCH?

Leverage is a valuable tool in your investment, but it can also work against you. If real estate value decreases several years in a row, you will find that you will be underwater on your mortgage, especially with zero or 5% down payment, as your debt is more than the value of your property. However, real properties are impact-free from inflation-free because of the land where you're rental home or building sits. Land never depreciates – only the buildings that sit on it. The land is the only asset that appreciates, and investors in real properties always take advantage of inflation because of their low cost. As long as you can hold on long enough until the market downturn reverses, you will never lose money in your real estate investment.

If you find the real estate market crashes and rents go down, it can eliminate your profit margin.

The solution here is to look for your balance between leverage and debt tolerance.

You may balance your risk by saving up to pay down your mortgage with the highest interest rate until it is paid off.

With sever paid-off homes and several mortgaged homes, these investments can provide you with solid returns.

By using leverage in real estate, you can use other people's money to increase profits. Depending on your investing strategy, owning rental properties is more superior to investing in stocks or Real Estate Investment Trust (REIT) because you don't need to use 100 percent of your money to own properties.

THE 7 ATTRIBUTES OF SUCCESSFUL LANDLORDS

A landlord may have its own set of ups and downs but still a rewarding job nonetheless. It is because landlords provide people with one of their necessities - shelter.

People usually think that a landlord should be well organized, caring, always on time, and excellent at negotiating and handling house-related matters.

Like anyone, a landlord is not perfect. Nonetheless, when one is willing to learn the ropes, qualities needed in business are developed along the way. The qualities of a successful landlord are not an exemption.

If you think that you do not have such qualities despite being a landlord, listed below are the key traits that you should learn and implement:

#1 ATTRIBUTE – CLEAR AND PRECISE COMMUNICATION

The primary key to developing a positive relationship with tenants is clear and precise communication. You should make sure to respond to concerns, inquiries, and questions as quickly as possible to avoid misunderstanding and frustration on the tenants' part. Whenever you make changes regarding rules or increasing rent, make sure to inform your tenants about it in advance. Sending emails regarding the matter may be good, but making a quick call or text can also come in handy. You can also try leaving a courteous note on your tenant's door, in case you cannot keep in touch with them using those three methods.

#2 ATTRIBUTE – PROFESSIONALISM

Building positive relationships with your tenants is essential, but try to maintain some distance. Becoming friends with them may look tempting, but it can be troublesome for business in the long run. After all, if you're friends with your tenants, they can test your flexibility with lease terms or become lax with their payments. As a landlord, you should treat your tenants as customers: it is good to be welcoming and friendly, but you should still professionally handle business-related matters.

#3 ATTRIBUTE – UNDERSTANDING

Policies and rules are crucial when putting up expectations and boundaries. Still, a good and successful landlord knows how to become flexible whenever unexpected matters arise— demonstrating a reasonable amount of understanding, e.g., delaying or waiving this month's rental payments to tenants who suddenly lost their jobs because of a financial crisis.

Nevertheless, it will earn you more respect from the tenants. It will also make them reciprocate more likely whenever your situations reverse. Keep in mind, however, that being understanding doesn't mean that you should become a pushover. Whenever a tenant asks for either leniency or exception, make sure to analyze the entire situation, lest it will create problems with other tenants in the future.

#4 ATTRIBUTE – WELL- ORGANIZED

A successful landlord keeps track of different matters affecting his business and should learn how to manage various tasks. Several issues, such as maintenance requests and leasing or renting rooms to new tenants, may require a lot of paperwork, including filing receipts for the tax season. You should have a structured system when organizing your files, so you don't have to look for every single document in the whole place. You can also make a reliable system that will keep track of your appointments.

Most landlords keep on forgetting how handy and helpful their smartphones can be when it comes to communication. It is the most convenient tool that a landlord can use when organizing things.

By installing spreadsheet software, you can easily document and store essential records before saving them in cloud-based storage such as Dropbox or Google Drive, or Microsoft OneDrive. You can also easily manage your time by using your smartphone's reminder and calendar features.

#5 ATTRIBUTE – WITH INTEGRITY

As a landlord, you may be able to easily rent out your rooms or house if you omit the so-called catch, such as untimely noises in the night, troublesome neighbours, faulty plumbing, and much more. However, your tenants must trust you since you will be keeping in touch with them regularly. Being transparent as much as possible is a must for every landlord.

By establishing a professional and positive relationship, tenants wouldn't feel that they are being cheated or taken advantage of. At the same time, they will even take good care of the house or rent since they won't like to be on the landlord's wrong side. Make sure to be open to your tenants' concerns and questions as much as possible. Doing this may somehow lead to a difficult conversation in the short term, but it will save you from trouble in the long run. For example, if there is a delay in the house maintenance or repair, try explaining everything to your tenants about the reason behind that situation.

#6 ATTRIBUTE – CONSISTENT

No matter what kind of landlord you are, you should be consistent in dealing with your tenants. For example, if you implement a no-excessive noise policy after ten o'clock in the evening, make sure that no one violates that policy, including you. Ensure your conditions in the lease contract as much as possible to prevent troubles in the future. As for emergencies or particular matters, make sure to talk the issue out with your tenants before creating and implementing new policies concerning those. Make sure that everyone is aware of whatever changes you make as much as possible.

#7 ATTRIBUTE – RESPECTFUL

Make sure to show respect even when you're dealing with disgruntled or rude tenants. Even if it's one-sided at first, a respectful relationship will eventually bring everyone to the same level of understanding. Keep in mind that tenants are humans just like you: their jobs could bring them stress and pressure, so having something they can call home is a sanctuary that protects them against those troubles, so expect them to get angry if they face a problem in their unit or house somehow.

Maintain professionalism, communicate clearly, and show respect and humility as much as possible. After all, paying disrespect back with disrespect won't lead to anything good.

Keep in mind that nobody is perfect. If you had shortcomings as a landlord, you don't have to beat yourself up because of it. Instead, make sure to change it and improve yourself for the better.

CHAPTER 2: WHICH REAL ESTATE VEHICLE WILL YOU DECIDE TO MASTER?

Now that you a ready to get into rental property investing, you must know the different investment vehicles and decide which one you will focus on. Take note that real estate investing takes time and is designed for the long term.

WHAT MAKES A GOOD PROPERTY INVESTMENT?

When you decide to get involved with real estate investments, you are most likely to earn wealth based on the risk you are taking while minimizing the time required in personally attending to the property.

When it comes to investing in rental property, making well-informed decisions is a must. As much as possible, your goal must be one or more of these.

THE INVESTMENT SHOULD BE MODERATELY RISKY

Real estate investment is extremely high-risk. However, real estate development, Tenant-in-common Investments, fixer-uppers, and real estate funds are much worse than just buying a rental property that you can manage yourself. Many of those investment strategies will make you never see your hard-earned money again because so many things could go wrong. So if you want to invest in real estate, buying rental properties is the best move with considerably lower risk compared to the rest.

IT MUST REQUIRE MUCH TIME OR MANAGING

Some real estate investments require much time or managing to make them smart investments. Examples of these include vacation rentals, college rentals, and low-quality properties in bad areas. Compared to these three, properties rented to decent credit profile tenants for as long as possible is much better since it requires little to no intervention right after the rental or lease contract is signed. Additionally, you can earn respect from your tenants over time as you address property-related matters as much as possible while establishing a good relationship with them. It may seem boring somehow but, the lesser the hassle brought by the rental property strategy, the better it becomes as time goes on.

IT SHOULD PROVIDE A STABLE CASH RETURNS

The main reason behind any investment is for you to have a passive income. It also applies to real estate investments. No matter what real estate investment strategy you're currently doing, it should be able to provide you with a decent cash-on-cash return. For example, invest your money in buying rental properties. You should be able to get a nice cash flow even after lessening everything, from taxes, mortgage payments, maintenance expenses, etc. To ensure your success, make sure to buy cash flow-positive properties, not negative ones.

RENTAL PROPERTY INVESTING

Pre-planning and homework are both required before investing in rental property to ensure its success. Consider the following before deciding to become a landlord:

LOCATION

The rental property's location plays a significant role in this investment strategy since it directly affects the tenants, who can rent the property. It is ideal to buy property in places where you can comfortably deal with the general population living in the area. The location also affects the value of the property as well as its appreciation potential. In other words, properties located in depressed or dangerous regions will not have the long-term market value appreciation compared to those found inside peaceful and better neighbourhoods.

PRICE AND FINANCING

It is necessary to know the actual fair market price of an investment property to prevent paying for overpriced properties. You can find the reasonable price from a comparable market analysis (CMA). You can determine a property market value through the capitalization rate method. You can do this by taking the property's net operating income (NOI) and dividing it by its market value. The result, expressed in percentage, should be equal or greater than the similar investment properties in the area to ensure that you can profit from it. When purchasing rental properties, you should thoroughly examine the cost and financing methods before making an offer on the property. Getting pre-approved for mortgages is also recommended to gain credibility, leverage, and clout with the seller.

PROPERTY'S CONDITION

A low-priced bargain investment property or a 'fixer-upper' may look good at first glance. However, it can be an expensive money pit when it comes to expenses involving repairs and upgrades. Address hidden defects of properties that are in poor condition first before applying the desired upgrades. The renovation cost and the lost rent opportunity cost should be taken into account, for it takes time to finish repairs and upgrades. Instead of buying a fixer-upper property, buying a more expensive but reliable 'turnkey' property is better for being cost-effective.

PROPERTY'S RENTAL INCOME

Some unethical sellers would 'inflate' the property's price by increasing rent.

One way of verifying actual rent is by sending mail 'estoppel letters' to tenants currently occupying the property.

On the other hand, the tenants will have to respond by confirming the actual rent they pay their landlord and conditions regarding their rental or lease agreements. It could also include the amount of security deposit that needs to be paid upfront upon sale of the property.

RENTAL PROPERTY MANAGEMENT

Whether you decide to do this personally or not, rental properties do need managers to stay operational. You either need to manage the property as the landlord or hire someone to do the managing work, which also means another set of expenses.

Factors that could affect your decision include:

- Rental property size

- Availability

- Management knowledge/skills

- Temperament for the job

If you find that managing work is not your thing, make sure to hire a reliable manager or avail services offered by a property management firm. Property management firms nowadays collect a part of the tenants' rent as their management fee. Nevertheless, keep in mind that there are also unethical property management firms, ones whom you should avoid at all costs.

MULTIFAMILY APARTMENT UNITS

It is usual for investors to add multifamily investing in their portfolio since it reduces vacancy rates while boosting one's income. Regarding real estate investing, single-family homes should be your focus since it generates the most significant passive income possible. Acquiring, renovating, and selling those are must-have skills when learning more about real estate investing.

MULTIFAMILY PROPERTIES

Multifamily refers to any residential property containing two or more housing units. Common examples of these are townhomes, duplexes, condominiums, and apartment complexes. With multifamily properties, new investors can find great investment opportunities. Some tenants prefer living in owner-occupied properties. Whether they want to live with the owner or not, it is still a great tool for building wealth.

INVESTMENT TIPS TO MINIMIZE UNNECESSARY LOSSES

Building a portfolio with a multifamily real estate investment is a good move but should be done carefully to minimize unnecessary losses. To do this, you must:

Calculate Your Cash Flow

You can determine whether the investment will be worthwhile or not by calculating your cash flow, which is done by subtracting the monthly mortgage from net operating income (NOI). The resulting number will be the actual income that is going inside your wallet. However, it is up to you whether that amount is considered to be worthwhile or not.

Find Your 50%

The surest way to scan through potential deals is by crunching the numbers and estimate how much income a certain multifamily property can make. Calculate the difference between the expected income and expenses. On the other hand, if you don't have access to such information in your neighbourhood, you can use the 50% rule, meaning that half of your estimated income becomes the expected income instead. The difference between the estimated income and estimated expenses becomes the net operating income (NOI).

Figure Out Your Cap Rate

The third important thing to consider before getting involved in multifamily real estate investments is none other than figuring out your capitalization (cap) rate. The capitalization rate determines how fast you are going to get your return on investment. It is necessary to consider two things here. First, the cap rate for a safe investment is about 1-2%. And second, the cap rate does not account for many factors. Also consider monthly NOI boosts, property value increases, and tax rates available for multifamily property owners.

To determine the cap rate, take the monthly NOI and multiply it by 12 to get the answer. After that, divide the resulting number by the property's present market value. The main thing to understand here is the fact that higher is not always better. It is because the higher the cap rate, the higher the risks and returns while a lower cap rate means lower risks and lower returns. The rule of the thumb, in this case, is to shoot for a cap rate in the 5-10% range since lower than those will not have enough yield. And numbers higher than those mean higher risks.

FACTORS TO LOOK FOR WHEN INVESTING IN MULTIFAMILY PROPERTIES

Window shopping for real estate can be done casually, but multifamily investing requires more attention. Investors should be diligent, locating a property below market value, analyzing and assessing its financial sensibility.

It takes a combination of things to ensure a quality real estate deal along with the hustle of finding properties. Usually, the search begins by locating a potential property, comparing market prices, long and short-term costs, and rental estimates. While this generally forecasts a figure of what investors can expect, it is up to them if they continue being diligent and refine the numbers to ensure success. Investing in multifamily properties requires more attention than other real estate deals and an investor's initial concern should be on the numbers. These figures will reveal its bottom line as well as expose its true value.

If you're interested in investing in multifamily properties, the checklist below will be of great help to you.

Location

The most important factor in real estate, especially multifamily properties, is none other than the location itself. The better the location, the more potential tenants it can have. And with more tenants, there will be more money to come. Investors should look for high-yield, high-growth areas where properties are in demand and a feasible location for multifamily properties.

Potential Income

The next thing to do is to determine how much income a property can generate. Craigslist or Rentometer.com is excellent sites for verifying rental prices and income, but investors should be diligent and consider everything.

Total Number of Units

Evaluate the property as a whole by considering the number of its units, as well as the number of rooms per unit.

Newbie investors should begin their real estate search into these three types of multifamily properties: duplex, triplex, and quadruplex. These properties offer the most substantial income with the least amount of risk for beginner investors and are more affordable in general.

Costs

Every situation differs when it comes to real estate financing, especially when it comes to multifamily properties. Investors may choose to live in one unit while renting out the other units, making them eligible for owner-occupied financing. In this case, the generated income from other units will be factored into the lender's qualifying ratio. When contemplating financing, investors should consider their overall credit score since this will significantly affect or influence the qualifying process.

Seller

When evaluating potential multifamily properties, the seller itself is an important factor that needs consideration. The property's purchase price depends on the seller and their intention or motivation behind selling the property. To say things simply, an investor should know who they are dealing with, especially when the property's price is somewhat questionable. Bank-owned properties, on the other hand, are dealt with differently compared to for-sale-by-owner properties. In this case, it has the potential for saving cost.

MOBILE HOMES

Real estate investing encompasses a broad spectrum of leasing spaces—from single or multifamily residential units to commercial high-rise spaces. Somewhere between this range is the unfamiliar niche, the **mobile home investing**.

A mobile home is a prefabricated building manufactured in a factory used as a permanent home or a temporary accommodation. It can be left permanently or semi-permanently in one place but can be moved under certain circumstances. Mobile homes are also known as:

- Recreational Vehicle (RV)

- Park home

- Trailer

- House trailer

- Trailer home

- Motor home

- Caravan

A mobile home provides living space just like a single-family unit or multifamily property. People have to pay rent to occupy a mobile home like they do to live in an apartment, a condo, or a residential home.

Mobile homes are an excellent investment. Unfortunately, many investors tend to overlook this real estate investing niche; but for the right investor, it can be an amazing and steady source of cash flow.

TYPES OF MOBILE HOME OWNERSHIP

Let us define what a mobile home investor is. There are two types of ownership:

The first type involves the **investor owning the lots where the renter can place their individual mobile units.** The place includes the land surrounding the lots, including the streets, swimming pools, utility systems, clubhouses, and other amenities. In this type of ownership, the tenant owns their home and only pays the right to inhabit the space where their home is situated plus the use of the facilities. This investing type involves investing in the "parks" rather than the mobile home units.

The second one involves the **investor owning both the unit and the land or park.** In this case, the tenant pays for both the use of the unit and the land, just like how other people rent an apartment unit.

REASONS TO CONSIDER MOBILE HOME

Your real estate portfolio may include a house or apartment as a rental property, but adding another niche can benefit you more. There are several reasons:

- Low financial entry point and quicker returns

- Lower taxes

- Less competition

- Lower renovation costs

- Mobile homes are highly marketable

- Will speed up your rental portfolio

- It can be done full-time or part-time

Many families have an annual income of $20,000. Although they come from a low-income bracket, they deserve a pleasant place to live. Also, some individuals are not fond of renting an apartment because they want a yard but cannot afford residential homes. You can provide affordable homes for these people through mobile home investing.

One of the most attractive aspects of mobile home investing is that they cost less compared to other rental property types.

Although a brand new mobile home may cost as much as a standard home, investors can choose second-hand mobile homes with a price tag lower than $10,000. They can also identify people who are willing to sell their mobile homes for about $1,000 or even less.

The low purchasing cost of acquiring a mobile home makes it easier for eager investors to start investing in real estate. With some effort, you can begin investing in mobile homes for as low as $5,000 or even lower.

Generally, a low initial investment gains a high potential return on investment (ROI); and this is true in mobile home investing. Let's say that you purchased a mobile home for merely $4,000 and net $200 per month after expenses and lot rent. You obtain a 60% return on investment (ROI).

With all these advantages, why there aren't many who are keen to invest in mobile homes? Unfortunately, many investors are not educated on investing in this real estate niche— but of course, this could be different.

DISADVANTAGES MOBILE HOME INVESTING

Again, like in other types of investment — real estate or not — investing in mobile homes has its downside:

MOBILE HOMES DO NOT APPRECIATE

One of the attractive things about real estate investing is that real estate almost always appreciates after quite some time. Even if a property does not appreciate much, it rarely loses its value. However, this is not true for mobile homes.

A manufactured home is likened to a vehicle when it comes to value— it depreciates. It is sporadic for someone to sell a mobile home for as much as its original price. A mobile home's cost is taken more as a liability than an asset, because you seldom get your original investment back. Understand that mobile investing is more about *cash flow*.

CHALLENGES IN FINANCING

It can be tricky getting a loan to acquire a mobile home since it is a high risk for a bank. Remember, mobile homes lose their value as soon as they are purchase. The bank also has to pay the lot rent if they have to repossess the home. However, mobile homes can be bought inexpensively; thus, you can purchase them without the bank's financial backup.

MOBILE HOMES REQUIRE HIGH MAINTENANCE

Most manufactured homes are not built in an equal standard as conventional homes. They are mass-produced in a factory and merely have to meet their standard requirements, not the city or county construction codes.

Mobile homes experience wear and tear over time at a quicker pace than their traditional counterparts. They require more maintenance than most types of house buildings.

LOT RENT

If your mobile home is "parked" in a rented lot, you are under the obligation to pay rent whether you have a tenant or not. The lot rent usually makes up the most portion of the rent payment. One month of lot rent may cost you as much as your mobile home rental income within two months.

HOW TO PROFIT FROM A SINGLE UNIT IN MOBILE HOMES INVESTING

There is no doubt that you can profit from mobile home investing, even if it is just a single mobile home unit. Here are several methods how you can do so:

OWNING THE HOME BUT NOT THE LAND

This situation happens when you either purchase an existing home unit in a park or move a mobile home into an existing park. In this case, you only have to pay the rent to the park owner, and they will take care of everything else, including the utilities, for you and your tenant. It simply means that you earn more cash flow. However, the downside is that moving a house requires you to follow the rules and pay fees associated with the event.

OWNING THE PARK BUT NOT THE HOMES

You can invest in mobile homes full-time or part-time. Owning the park sans the homes is highly recommended for those investors who opt to do this investing type as their part-time jobs. In this case, your advantages include having to take care only of the park. You do not need to worry about individual repairs for mobile homes. You can also supervise them from a distance. Raising the rent after purchasing a park also increases your cash flow. The drawback of this setup is that there is less cash flow because you only charge a lot of rent.

OWNING BOTH THE HOMES AND THE PARK

If you own both the land and structure, then you have the best of both worlds. You can collect everything, which simply means a greater cash flow. If you are looking for a potential land to build the park, try to look for one that has access to city water or sewage. The disadvantage of this option is that it requires a considerable amount of capital. You also have to do the repairs and maintenance on the mobile homes and the park.

OWNING THE PARK & SELLER FINANCING THE HOMES

In case you own the park and resort to seller financing the homes, it is crucial to have a periodic inspection detailed down into the lease contract. This way, you can monitor your rental properties. You must also consider hiring a property management company.

This setup's benefits involve owning the park, selling homes on a note, and receiving continuous cash flow. On the other hand, you may experience high turnover because when a new buyer purchases a park and updates the rules, the tenants may consider moving out.

SEMI-DEVELOPMENT DEALS

You can purchase a piece of land together with an old mobile home on it in this scenario. Replace the old structure and sell the land and new mobile home as a package. Usually, in this case, utilities are already placed as part of the package.

LAND HOME DEALS

The land home deal is a form of seller financing. With this strategy, an individual borrows money from a lender. That person may make payments to the seller or real estate owner until the purchase price is paid entirely.

MOBILE HOME INVESTING STRATEGIES

Your real estate investing goals will dictate your investment strategy. Your options may include *a wholesale deal, renting,* and *flipping.*

Some mobile home investors favor investing in older-looking trailers because of several reasons:

- Quick returns

- Small investment

- Low risk

- Obtaining the best for your money

They deal with the seller to obtain the old trailer for free and renovate it for a profit.

Usually, you could charge an equivalent rent of a one-bedroom apartment to the rent of a two-bedroom mobile home.

To give you further ideas, here are three types of mobile homes along with their cost:

Single-Wide

Single-wide mobile homes are usually 14-feet to 18-feet wide and 52-feet and 80-feet long. It houses a living room, kitchen, one or two bathrooms, and at least two bedrooms. It costs around $57,600 to $64,000.

Double-Wide

Double-wide mobile homes range from 28-feet to 36-feet wide and 52-feet to 80-feet long. On average, it houses two to three bedrooms, two bathrooms, a living room, and an eat-in kitchen. A unit can cost as much as $110,300 to $122,900.

Of course, you can rent it out for double the occupancy and price. However, keep in mind that since they are transported in two sections and then installed together, the moving cost is more expensive than a single-wide.

Triple-Wide or Multi-Wide

This class is also known as multi-section manufactured homes. It is transported in three sections, making its moving cost more expensive than the double-wide mobile homes. It can range from two to six bedrooms and four bathrooms.

Triple-wide or multi-wide mobile homes can be pretty difficult to distinguish since they usually have diverse and asymmetrical floor plans. They primarily run from 2,000 to 3,000 square feet in size.

MOBILE HOME INVESTING PURCHASE PROCESS

The purchase process for mobile homes can significantly differ from purchasing an apartment or a traditional house. For this reason, you need to check with your local registry of motors and get the guidelines. Nevertheless, here are the essentials when purchasing a used mobile home the title for the home (including VIN, brand, year, and manufactured home labels), bill of sale, and application form for the new title.

CONTRACT OF PURCHASE ISSUES IN MOBILE HOME TITLES

When purchasing a mobile home from someone, you may encounter title issues. Here are some samples and how you may address them:

LOST MOBILE HOME TITLE BUT STILL UP FOR SALE

Sometimes, you get attracted by a mobile home that you believe has potential. Unfortunately, the title is lost. You may wonder if:

- The seller is actually telling the truth or not

- The mobile home is legal or not

- The title is just faded or really lost

The solution is quite simple: Go to the registry and request a duplicate title. If it is merely lost or faded, then you will surely obtain a copy of the title.

THE MOBILE HOME IS UP FOR SALE BUT HAS INCORRECT OWNER AND NO TITLE

When you encounter this issue, there is a chance that the transaction was legal. However, the new owner failed to change the title. For this, you need to look for the original owner. It can be difficult, and if the person is already deceased, you will have to find the estate's executor.

You can also skip the tracing if the seller can provide a bill of sale signed by the original owner. This is enough proof for transaction and ownership.

MOBILE HOME INVESTING LEADS

If you have decided to take mobile home investing as a niche and would like to start, how can you acquire leads?

First, you have to visit several mobile home parts to get acquainted with the industry you want to join. Establish connections as you meet new people in the business. In this type of investing business, one-on-one interaction is a must, especially when dealing with an older seller. You may be thinking that direct mail may work on this niche, but you are mistaken. While the idea of sending mail may work for other types of investing niches, it does not typically work with mobile homes.

Look for a network of mobile home investors and agents, and connect with them. Introduce yourself as someone keen on buying mobile homes. You will be surprised how this traditional method will work for your endeavors.

If you are digital savvy, optimize your lead generation on platforms such as Facebook and Craigslist.

AIRBNB UNITS

It is pretty popular with real estate investors who want to generate high profits to purchase and manage Airbnb investment properties. But, if you want high profits, getting Airbnb rental income will surely make you sweat before you earn it. As an investor for this type of real estate property, you need to consider numerous factors that you will need as an Airbnb host before you take your shot at investing in short-term rentals.

WHAT IS AIRBNB AND HOW IT WORKS

Many pioneering investors are interested in investing in this investment strategy type. Unfortunately, they are not knowledgeable on how they would proceed with their desired investment. We will cover all the essential aspects of buying and managing Airbnb investment property.

To start with, you should determine what type of Airbnb investor you want to be: do you want to be a passive or an active host? In case you want to become a passive investor, being an Airbnb host might not be the ideal type of investment for you.

Furthermore, we will tackle:

- Type of property management application for an Airbnb investment property

- Considerations when you buy a property that you will lease as a short-term rental

- Rental income

- Monthly investment cost

- Property listing on the Airbnb rental market

When it comes to investment property renting, there are two popular strategies that you could choose from:

- Airbnb

- Traditional investing

If you want to be an active investor, Airbnb rental would be a suitable investment strategy for you. Active investor means that you (as the landlord) are willing to spend your time and effort on your rental property. You will be the one who would personally see to it that your guests are provided with the best experience possible and maintain the rental constantly.

In contrast with Airbnb, you are a passive investor with traditional investing. What makes the landlord a passive investor when it comes to this strategy is that your constant presence is not needed to suit your tenants once your property has been rented. You will just wait for and receive the monthly rental payment even if you do nothing in particular. However, if there happens to be a maintenance problem or your proposal needs to be repaired, that is the time that your assistance is needed. Unlike Airbnb rentals, traditional investing properties will not require constant maintenance.

PROS AND CONS OF INVESTING IN AIRBNB

Whether you have stayed in an Airbnb rental for vacation or have just heard about the lucrative possibilities of owning a sought-after short-term property, including Airbnb homes in your portfolio is a smart way to boost your passive income.

Using the Airbnb platform to rent properties can be a lucrative real estate investment strategy, but it also has challenges.

IT MAY BE MORE LUCRATIVE THAN TRADITIONAL RENTING

A solidly-booked Airbnb rental may be more profitable than renting the property to a single, long-term tenant. That is because you are usually able to charge more on a nightly basis.

In Seattle, for example, the average apartment rent is $2,000 per month. If the tenant signed a 12-month lease, this figure translates to $24,000 annual gross income.

But what if you went the Airbnb route? According to AirDNA, the average daily rate for an Airbnb rental in Seattle is about $150 with the average number of occupancy days is about 270 per year, making it possible for a home rental owner to rake in $40,500 in gross revenue from the rental.

That's $16,000 more than you would earn through traditional renting.

These numbers only reflect gross revenue: Your actual income could be higher if the property appreciates and your net revenue could be lower because of various expenses incurred for operating your rental property business.

IT CAN PROVIDE YOU DIVERSIFIED TENANTS

With conventional renting, you are betting your entire investment on one tenant. There is no problem if the tenant stays for an extended period and financially stable. But if they ever miss rent payments or vanish in the night, your income takes an immediate hit since it is hard to find a replacement tenant immediately.

With Airbnb rental, you will have different tenants, and the percentage that a tenant cannot pay is out of the question since they are required to pay in advance. However, there are many restrictions imposed on Airbnb depending on your location. In someplace, you can only rent it out unless the property is your place of residence.

In San Francisco, a residence is defined as the place where you stay for at least 275 nights a year. Your business can be considered illegal once you have more than 90 nights of unhosted rentals. Simply put, being an absentee landlord is not allowed.

Nowadays, many cities are still considering regulating short-term rentals or not, making Airbnb risky for investors who wish to indulge in this type of rental property investment.

IT ENTAILS HIGHER EXPENSES

When renting out a single-family rental property, the required time involves in managing it is very minimal. A conscientious tenant will pay bills regularly, keep the place clean, mow the lawn, and stock the cupboards. You are only required to handle issues and emergency situation that may arise from time to time in addition to maintaining your property.

Conversely, operating an Airbnb property is more labour-extensive, for you have to ensure that your place is clean and in order all the time to get ready for accommodation. There are also things you will likely need to provide to a single tenant, such as high-quality furniture, decor, appliances, and amenities.

The first impression counts, especially in Airbnb rentals. It's one way to gather referrals and promote guest's loyalty. If you want to impress your guests, provide them with an unforgettable, and they will surely spread the word to others about this. Provide them with additional conveniences, and you will reap its returns in the long run. Here are examples of little conveniences you can give away.

Food

Providing some snacks or stocking some necessities in the kitchen like pastries, candies, eggs, coffee, and other beverages can make your guest's stay enjoyable.

Cable TV, Wi-Fi, and Other Entertainment Facilities

Airbnb tenants usually expect comfort and convenience during their stay that providing an Airbnb unit complete facilities including TC, Wi-Fi, etc., can be added sources of enjoyment to your guests. With such facilities, you can expect a higher rental payment.

Hiring a management company and a cleaning service handle all these will make your job easier. Nevertheless, these are added operating costs.

In many locations, Airbnb homeowners withhold taxes from tenants to remit to appropriate taxing authorities. But there are locations where you have to pay your tax manually.

SUCCESS MAY BE GRADUAL

Like any other investments or business venture, success doesn't come easy. It is the same with Airbnb rentals. You can't expect to book tenants as soon as you set up your account with the platform. You have to build your reputation online before you can get your first tenant. This is why you have to provide them with an incredibly amazing experience during their stay so they will give you good reviews online. The higher rating they will give you, the higher probability you will have to get more bookings potential renters in the future.

While still starting to build up your rental business, to attract renters, offer low rent and gradually increase it as you receive good reviews and ratings from previous guests. You may also offer incentives to encourage extended stay in your property especially if your property is not located in the metropolis. You cannot assume rental income to come in rolling quickly even when you have a great unit in a prime location.

INCOME COULD BE IRREGULAR

If you own a property and rent it to a single tenant, you may be able to keep that tenant on a long-term lease and collect rent each month. It can be a steady source of income that is passive. Airbnb rentals may be far more inconsistent. While your property may be available for 365 days in a year, you are most likely to have many days where it is unoccupied. To prepare the property or unit for the next guest, you may prefer to have it vacant in a day or two between bookings.

The issue of vacant dates can worsen if you live in a locality that restricts the number of days you can rent out an Airbnb unit. If you are willing to go all out in attracting more tenants and provide them with a pleasurable experience during their stay, Airbnb can be a lucrative investment. Make sure that you have enough patience and do your research before plunging into Airbnb rental investing.

BUYING YOUR PROPERTY

Have you decided already if Airbnb will be your real estate investment? If yes, let's talk about the next step: purchase your property. You might say that making a purchase is easy if you've got money, however, the success of your Airbnb rental investment will also depend on other factors. Analytics is also important but the location of your property investment is more significant. Be mindful of choosing and purchasing your investment property. To have higher Airbnb occupancy rates and generate a positive cash flow, find a place that will be attractive for tourists. It may be places that are interesting to visit or ideal vacation spots.

Another good point is if the place is holding many business meetings. People from different places will meet up there and would look for a place to stay.

Also, look for a property with a quiet and safe neighbourhood. Properties that are easily accessible to supermarkets and public transportation will also be plus points for your property investment.

MANAGING YOUR AIRBNB PROPERTY

If you want success for your Airbnb investment property, high-quality property management is crucial. Why? There are Airbnb reviews. These are ratings and comments that your guests give about your property. Airbnb reviews can contribute to the make-or-break point of your Airbnb property since they can either attract more visitors to your rental property or give a negative view that will reduce your bookings. This is exactly the main reason why you (as the host) should try your best to manage your rental property.

The basic rules about Airbnb rentals are that you make sure that your guests are invited to a clean property. You should provide them with enough supplies like clean towels, bed sheets, extra pillows or blankets. Check toiletries and kitchen supplies after each visit and if needed, restock. Examples of basic supplies are toilet paper, soap, shampoo, paper towels, sugar, salt, coffee, etc.

If you aim to score higher on these reviews, organize activities, prepare city maps for your guests, prepare meals and so on. Improve your performance by being creative and you will be guaranteed success for scoring high on Airbnb occupancy rates.

RENTAL INCOME AND MONTHLY INVESTMENT COSTS

To know and ensure that you are generating a positive cash flow, your Airbnb rental earnings (cash inflow) should be higher than your investment costs (cash outflow) for each month. Don't forget, as based on analytics, it won't guarantee the hottest destinations will also be the highest profit baggers. Why? The reason is that such places will probably be more expensive and so will your costs increase. Another thing is, if your location is a hot spot, you will most likely have higher competition, so your rental charge will also get limited. In short, you will have difficulty in getting a positive cash flow from your rental property.

LISTING YOUR RENTAL PROPERTY (RENTAL CHARGE)

Listing your rental property deals with how much your charge will be for the rent when you start promoting your property. Of course, you would aim for the highest occupancy rates possible once you enlist your property on the market for short-term rentals. To do this, put into consideration the price you will charge your guests per night. It is also advisable to check on how much your competitors are charging for their rentals. Check also the charge rates of motels and hotels nearby. Avoid charging too high for your rentals because it will reflect on your Airbnb occupancy rates and you will probably have low occupancy.

Furthermore, when you are presenting your rental property, get creative and share something unique.

MARKETING STRATEGIES TO ENSURE SUCCESS

Nowadays, competition in the short-term rental market becomes tighter as the market itself expands rapidly. If your business investment falls along the Airbnb lines, you should implement a consistent marketing strategy that would put your business apart from the others.

You should indeed aim to provide your guests with an amazing experience during their stay in your place. However, this is no longer the only factor that would make you advance from your competitors and give your occupancy rate a boost. This is because as the vacation rental industry becomes more progressive, hosts face the difficulty of making themselves distinguished above the others in their field of competition. So, if you want your business to be on top of the game, you need to have an Airbnb marketing strategy that is thoroughly and carefully planned.

To start with an effective marketing strategy for your Airbnb, you should analyze first the things that make your competitors secure their bookings and identify their weak points. Use the information that you got to craft your marketing strategies and take advantage of their weak points. Also, listed below are the best marketing practices that when applied, can be your arsenal to gain the lead in your industry of short-term rentals.

CREATE YOUR BRAND

What will be your point of difference from the others in the marketplace? Of course, your brand name! Start with establishing the brand of your Airbnb business by giving it a name and making your own logo. Then, use it on all your vacation rental platforms and your social media accounts for streamlining your digital marketing strategy.

Establishing your brand will be your foundation as it not only becomes an effective marketing strategy but also builds loyalty and trust in your business over time. Your vacation rental business brand will make your guests remember your place easily. It will also help them in finding you faster when they want to stay in your place again.

ADVERTISE WITH FACEBOOK

Based on the latest data, when travelers plan for their trip, 52% of them look on social media for recommendations and 42% of Facebook posts are travel stories. Put these two together, and you will find a perfect spot where you could promote your Airbnb rental- Facebook.

Incorporate your marketing strategy with Facebook by making a Facebook business page for your property. Whenever you post something on your page, be sure to link back your posts to your listings on your Airbnb platforms.

Also, use your Facebook business page to share content that can be helpful to travellers, such as tips and recommendations.

Lastly, attract more followers and be more engaging with your page by running a paid Facebook Ads campaign. Facebook will contact you on your business page to tell you more specific details about a paid ad campaign and its cost for boosting your post.

USE INSTAGRAM IN YOUR MARKETING CAMPAIGN

There's no question that Facebook could provide stellar results for your marketing strategy. However, Instagram could give you more viewers, especially if you plan to reach the younger generation of the audience. To prove this point, 500 million people are using Instagram daily, including millennials and Gen Z travellers. So, if you want more for your audience, get Instagram to reach them.

Furthermore, Instagram is a platform that deals more on the visual side- videos and photos. You can showcase the full beauty of your property investment there as long as you make sure that you follow the best marketing practices by making all your videos and photos look pro.

Lastly, if you could get amazing photos with the help of a professional photographer, it's better to invest in quality photos of your properties. Otherwise, if you want to save cash, you could also try to learn to enhance your photos using smartphone apps such as Lightroom, VCSO, Instasize, Afterlight, etc. Through these apps, you can make great content yourself on your Instagram account.

ESTABLISH A YOUTUBE CHANNEL FOR YOUR BRAND

More than just the most popular video site, YouTube is also next to Google as the largest search engine. There are 1.9 billion YouTube users all over the globe with the continual growth of video content.

If you want help in personalizing your brand, creating your YouTube channel is another excellent Airbnb marketing strategy. It should focus on videos that will feature your properties alongside helpful traveller tips. You should also craft engaging content that will help travellers know more about your place. For instance, videos about the top attractions that your property offers and what makes your site a must-visit should be the contents of your videos.

Aside from this, your strategy content should be really valuable to travellers, like recommendations or insider tips from someone extremely familiar with your place.

To have the best chances of becoming popular among your viewers, the titles of your videos must provide a list, like "Top 5 Beaches ..." or "Top 10 To-Do Things in ..." As your content grows more popular, the higher rank, it will get in the YouTube search results. Also, your rental property marketing strategy should focus on building YouTube subscribers for your channel.

CONNECT WITH THE RIGHT INFLUENCERS

Another well-known and effective Airbnb digital marketing strategy is collaborating with popular influencers that could boost your vacation rental investment. Your business could gain exposure through the aid of Instagram or YouTube travel bloggers.

But then, if you want satisfying results from a partnership with an influencer, do these things first:

Identify the Right Influencers

Ensure that your business and influencer match by knowing your audience thoroughly and understanding the audience of the influencer. Take note of the age and the potential interests of the influencer's followers as well.

Set Clear Goals and Objectives

Plan and choose the aspects of your rental business that you would want to get promoted. And, don't forget how you can determine if your ad campaign is successful or not.

Lay Out Your Terms

Your written contract with the influencer should include the following terms and conditions:

- What you will give the influencer in return for your business's promotion

- Minimum requirements that the influencer must fulfill to get compensated for their efforts

- Duration of marketing campaign

- How to end the collaboration when things didn't go as planned

Since finding the right influencer/s for your short-term rental business will most probably be the most time-consuming of all your Airbnb marketing strategies, plan carefully to get the best results.

LOCAL PARTNERSHIPS AND WHAT YOU CAN GET FROM THEM

Local partnerships or collaborations with other businesses such as amusement parks, local restaurants, equipment rental companies and the likes can offer a unique value when crafted in your Airbnb marketing strategy. Such business relationships are something that most of your competitors won't take part in. However, they can also help in advertising your business to the locals.

You can offer discounts and special offers to your guests with the help of your local partners. This will enable both ventures (you and your partners) to establish joint, mutual and profitable businesses in your area. It will also make your guests appreciate their bookings with you as it will help them save money using local special offers while staying at your place.

CREATIVITY IS THE KEY TO GET TO SUCCESS

What gets you ahead of everyone in the Airbnb field is a well-crafted online marketing strategy that oozes creativity. You could attract more guests and establish your position as a top Airbnb host if you exert more efforts and provide quality value to your audience.

Enhance your Airbnb listing through ads and promotions so you could benefit from securing more bookings and enjoy a revenue increase.

A BRIEF BACKGROUND ON AIRBNB

From recent decades until today, platforms like Airbnb that introduce home-sharing have become highly attractive, eventually leading to the surging popularity of short-term rentals. You might think that short-term renting has only been popularized recently, but contrary to what most people believe, this practice is undoubtedly done even before home-sharing platforms ever existed. Only it was known under the name vacation rentals.

Vacation rentals came to the scene when people found the inexpensive, alternative way of escaping their homes to enjoy a holiday without having to book in a hotel. Around the 1950s, this became a customary tradition for many. Vacation homes for rent (short vacation rentals) advertisements and listings started to appear in the newspapers.

2008 was the year when Airbnb started as a small pioneering company in San Francisco that offered guests a single room booking in a home of a host and accepted payment through credit cards over the internet. It was the first company to have that unique offering, unlike others who offer a variety of short-term hotel bookings and vacation rentals.

Airbnb experienced exponential growth through the years – from 2,500 listings and 10,000 users as of March 2009 to the current estimated number of around 6 million listings and 150 million users all over the globe. Aside from that, with Airbnb Experiences, this company has begun its expansion outside the short-term rental industry. With Airbnb Experiences, they allowed their users to host unique events, city tours and classes available for anyone who wants to sign up through their website.

THE FUTURE OF SHORT-TERM RENTALS

As of the past decades, the short-term rental industry has expanded largely, mainly, through the help of Airbnb's concept of convenient and profitable home-sharing. Because of that, Marriott International and other leading hotel companies are preparing for their service expansion to the home rental space by bringing 2,000 upscale homes of their Homes and Villas to the market for short-term rental.

As for Airbnb, recently purchased Rockefeller Centre suites are being readied that would offer their guests a more curated hotel experience.

These strategies coming from both sectors of short-term rentals and home-sharing give a vivid idea that the hotels and accommodation sector has been already disrupted. Only the test of time could prove if traditional hotels are going to keep up with the said industry's evolution happening at present.

Alternate accommodation pioneers such as Lyric, Stay Alfred, and Sonder have been seen rising in the short-term rental space.

They have been raising funds and attracting attention with such rapid progression for their upscale but affordable suites and boutique hotels for travellers.

As short-term rentals become more popular with Airbnb platform of casual home-sharing, companies and professional property managers become visible in the short-term rental space as they help meet the rising standards of more incoming customers. Independent hosts are now turning to co-hosting companies such as *Hostnfly*, *Luckey* by Airbnb and *Vacasa* so that they could still meet the rising competition in the short-term rental market with its continuous offering expansions and quality stay improvements.

New Competitors in the Short-Term

It's easy to say that the competition in the short-term rental industry has become tighter because of new competitors in the field:

- The entry of Rental Market through hotels gained some attention

- Different Airbnb competitors working on getting a portion of the market

- OYO (an Indian accommodation giant) receiving investment from Airbnb

- *Sonder* and *Stay Alfred* offer alternative stays for those who want the comfort and charms of a vacation rental but with the hotel's professional service.

The companies mentioned above aim to provide their guests' purpose-built and well-designed suites to provide much better and more flexible accommodation that comes at affordable prices. Spaces are prepared and managed professionally, so that possible friction that may come from inexperienced hosting on platforms like Airbnb may be reduced avoided.

It is quite apparent that these companies are raising millions of dollars in their industry. It also means that short-term rental demand is continuously rising.

It is quite popular with real estate investors who want to generate high profits to purchase and manage Airbnb investment properties. But, if you wish to gain higher yields, getting Airbnb rental income will surely make you sweat before you earn it. As an investor for this type of real estate property, you need to consider numerous factors that you will need as an Airbnb host before you take your shot at investing in short-term rentals.

GETTING STARTED WITH AIRBNB

Many pioneering investors are interested in investing in this investment strategy type. Unfortunately, they are not knowledgeable on how they would proceed with their desired investment.

To start with, you should determine what type of Airbnb investor you want to be.

Do you want to be a passive or an active host? If you want to become a passive investor, being an Airbnb host might not be the ideal type of investment for you.

Furthermore, we will tackle:

- Type of property management applicable to an Airbnb investment property

- Considerations when you buy a property that you will lease as a short-term rental

- Rental income

- Monthly investment cost

- Property listing on the Airbnb rental market

AIRBNB INVESTOR VS. TRADITIONAL INVESTOR

When it comes to investment property renting, there are two popular strategies that you could choose from:

- Airbnb

- Traditional investing

If you want to be an active investor, Airbnb rentals would be a suitable investment strategy for you. Active investor means that you are willing to spend your time and effort on your rental property. You will be the one who would personally see to it that your guests are provided with the best experience possible and maintain the rental constantly.

In contrast with Airbnb, you are a passive investor with traditional investing. What makes the landlord a passive investor when it comes to this strategy is that your constant presence is not actually needed to cater to your tenant's needs once your property is rented. You will just wait and receive the rental payment even if you do nothing in particular.

However, if there happens to be a maintenance problem or your property needs some repairs, that is the time your assistance is needed. Unlike Airbnb rentals, traditional investing properties will not require constant maintenance.

MANAGING YOUR AIRBNB PROPERTY

If you want success for your Airbnb investment property, high-quality property management is crucial. Why? Airbnb guests are providing reviews online. These are ratings and comments that your guests give about your property. Airbnb reviews can contribute to the make-or-break point of your Airbnb property since they can either attract more visitors to your rental property or give a negative view that will reduce your bookings. This is exactly the main reason why you (as the host) should try your best to manage your rental property.

The basic rule about Airbnb rentals is that you make sure that your rental property is clean and in order. You should provide your guests with enough supplies like clean towels, bedsheets, extra pillows or blankets. Check toiletries and kitchen supplies after each visit and, if needed, restock. Examples of basic supplies are toilet paper, soap, shampoo, paper towels, sugar, salt, coffee, etc.

If you aim to score higher on these reviews, organize activities, prepare city maps for your guests, prepare meals and so on. Improve your performance by being creative, and you will be guaranteed success for scoring high on Airbnb occupancy rates.

PURCHASING YOUR PROPERTY

Have you decided already if Airbnb will be your real estate investment? If yes, let's talk about the next step: purchasing your property.

You might say that making a purchase is easy if you have money. However, the success of your Airbnb rental investment will also depend on many factors. Although analytics is important, the location of your property investment is more significant. So, be really mindful of choosing and purchasing your investment property. To have higher Airbnb occupancy rates and generate cash flow, find a place that is attractive to tourists. It may be places that are interesting to visit or ideal vacation spots.

Another good point is if the place is holding many business meetings. People from different places will meet up there and would look for a place to stay.

Also, look for a property with a quiet and safe neighbourhood. Properties that are easily accessible to supermarkets and public transportation will also be plus points for your property investment.

RENTAL INCOME AND MONTHLY INVESTMENT COSTS

To know and ensure that you are generating a positive cash flow, your Airbnb rental earnings (cash inflow) should be higher than your investment costs (cash outflow) for each month. Don't forget, as based on analytics, it won't guarantee the hottest destinations will also be the highest profit baggers. Why? The reason is that such places will probably be more expensive and so will your costs increase. Another thing is, if your location is a hot spot, you will most likely have higher competition so your rental charge will also get limited. In short, you will have difficulty in getting a positive cash flow from your rental property.

Another thing to discuss is, of course, how much you charge for rent when listing the property.

LISTING YOUR RENTAL PROPERTY (RENTAL CHARGE)

Now, let's deal with how much will be your rental charge when you start to enlist your property. Of course, you would aim for the highest occupancy rates possible once you enlist your property on the market for short-term rentals. To do this, put into fateful consideration the price you will charge your guests per night. It is also advisable to check on how much your competitors within your area charge for their rentals. Check also the charge rates of motels and hotels nearby. Don't charge too high for your rentals because it will reflect on your Airbnb occupancy rates – lest you will have low occupancy.

Furthermore, be creative when presenting your rental property. Make sure to something unique.

TIPS FOR ACHIEVING A HIGH AIRBNB OCCUPANCY RATE

Airbnb is a competitive business. By utilizing it, you are trying to obtain guests from all over the country to choose your property over hundreds of other properties in your vicinity. In other words, you need to differentiate yourself from others to make sure that your stay on the top of the pyramid. To achieve this, you have to the following:

BECOME A SUPER HOST

Achieving a super host status in one's Airbnb profile means that they managed to accomplish four things in just a year.

- Maintaining a 90% positive response rate

- Having a 5-star rating on 80% of the reviews

- Hosting at least ten trips

- Completing every customer reservation without cancellation

This status means a high occupancy rating on your Airbnb property while making a name for yourself on the Airbnb platform at the same time.

SHOOT FANTASTIC PHOTOS OF THE PROPERTY

The better the picture, the better it sells. In other words, if your property's photos look great, the more attention it will get. In obtaining bookings, photos are the most crucial factor, and people make judgments according to what they see. Airbnb offers free access to professional photography depending on one's location. By hiring a professional photographer, you can draw potential tenants to your property. So see to it that their shots showcase the best features of your house, which will create entice and ensure your clients that they will get the best experience staying in your property. You likewise post a welcoming photo of yourself to create an ambience that emits hospitality.

GIVE YOUR GUESTS THE BEST EXPERIENCE

Make sure to provide your guests what they want and tell them whatever they want to hear. Customize your property based on the type of guests you want to target. Add small accommodations to let them know that you think of their well-being. You can also print a list of restaurants, amusement centers, and shops in your vicinity so your renters can find them with ease. Your guests may have a better experience even without your intervention if your property is within the metropolis.

On the other hand, having your property in a small town requires you to put extra effort into keeping tabs on the usual places of interest in your vicinity.

KEEP THINGS CLEAN AND IN ORDER

No guest would want to live inside a dirty place for as long as they can manage it. No one will also use things such as a dirty microwave or air conditioner. It makes cleaning an essential and tedious part of rental property investing. You can either save money by cleaning the property on your own or hire a cleaning company and charge a cleaning fee to your customers.

Some cleaning companies choose to affiliate with Airbnb like Guesty, Handy, and Pillow. These companies also offer coupons and deals depending on the client. They make money as you steadily increase your Airbnb property's occupancy rate, ensuring that they have enough cleaning jobs to do.

INVEST IN YOUR PROPERTY

Keep yourself organized at all times. Always keep marks on your calendar updates to avoid double bookings or whenever your properties are unavailable. And whenever you accept a booking, make sure to serve your guests well. Keep in mind that your guests' response rate is the pivotal key to improve your Airbnb occupancy rate.

Maintaining your profile and property is part of the routine, so make a schedule and fulfill your tasks on time. On the other hand, if you don't have enough time, you may hire a property management company to do the job for a fee.

SET A REASONABLE PRICE

Airbnb property rents are way cheaper than traditional lodging, so people prefer using it more, especially if they only want to rent a property for a short time. In other words, if you set prices too high, no one will dare to use your property, no matter how great the experience your property can give them. At the same time, if guests can save money while renting your property, you may get good, if not excellent, reviews. These reviews will help your business in the long run.

AVOID LEGAL ISSUES

Even if you are using Airbnb, ensure that your property still adheres to your country's regulations and laws regarding rental properties. Make sure to communicate with your neighbours regularly to avoid misunderstandings. If your city or town has restrictions on the number of days one can rent out their properties, make sure that you take note of those to avoid unnecessary penalties.

COMMERCIAL REAL ESTATE

Commercial Real Estate is a property that is leased for retail and other business-related purposes, which is to provide a workspace rather than a space to live. It is often leased to tenants for income-generating activities.

Commercial Real Estate Investing involves the purchase and development of properties that aim to house commercial tenants. Unlike residential real estate, commercial real estate properties rented out, allowing investors to collect rent from businesses that occupy and use commercial space. Included under the commercial property is the raw land purchased for developing commercial property.

Commercial real estate is generally categorized into four classes based on their function.

- Retail
- Office space
- Multi-family rental
- Industrial use

COMMERCIAL ESTATE INVESTING PROS AND CONS

Residential and commercial properties could offer you good investment opportunities. But if you want to gain more financial reward, commercial properties would be the type of investment opportunity for you rather than investing your money in residential properties (e.g., single-family homes or rental apartments). However, you are going to fare with more risks upon investing in commercial properties. Thus, you need to understand fully the pros and cons that come with commercial property investing. Then, choose if it's the right investment opportunity for you or not.

When you manage commercial properties, you will find certain variations for handling each property type. For a more straightforward illustration, let's take a single-story commercial retail building like a community strip mall as an example and look closely at the pros and cons of investing in it.

REASONS WHY YOU SHOULD INVEST IN COMMERCIAL PROPERTY

INCOME POTENTIALS

It is the best advantage that you could get for investing in commercial properties versus residential rentals. Typically, you could get an annual return off the purchase price that ranges from 6-12% depending on the location, the current economy, and some other external factors (e.g., pandemic). That is a lot higher than what you could get for a single-family home property that ranges typically from 1-4% only.

Professional Relationships

Small business owners tend to protect their livelihood as they take pride in their businesses. Most commercial property owners are Limited Liability Companies (LLC) that operate their properties as a business. Because of this, landlords and tenants have a more inclined business-to-business customer relationship that keeps professional and courteous interactions between both parties.

Public Eye on Your Investment Property

Both retail tenants and the property owner have aligned interests in maintaining and improving the quality of the property. It is because retail/ commercial tenants need to keep their store and storefront as it affects their business in general. It is also normal for property owners to improve their property and the value of their investment.

Operation Hours are Limited

Most businesses close at night, so it's easy to say that you also have to work whenever they are in operation. Unlike residential rentals, you can have a good night's sleep without bothering to bar emergency calls at night in case of fire alarms or break-ins. Your tenants would be notified by the alarm company in case something happened during the night. You also won't receive midnight calls because a tenant lost a key or needed repair for something.

Price Evaluations are More Objective

Residential properties tend to become subjected to emotions before they evaluate the price rent for the property. On the other hand, commercial property owners could request the income statement of the present owner to assess prices and determine the rent price based on that information. If the owner has a knowledgeable broker, they could set the asking price at a fee where the investor can earn the prevailing cap rate of the area for the commercial property type they are looking forward to investing in (retail, industrial, office, etc.).

Triple Net Leases

Though there are nuances to triple net leases, still the basic concept is that the property owner (you) are not responsible for paying for the property expenses (as with residential real estate). Your lessee should handle all property expenses directly together with the real estate taxes, and you will have to pay for your mortgage.

Walgreens, Starbucks, and CVS are some of the companies that sign these leases because they want to keep up with their brand and maintain a look. In short, they manage the cost for you, and you, as an investor, have the lowest maintenance income producers for your income stream.

Usually, triple nets are not available for smaller businesses, and strip malls have various net leases. However, the leases that they provide are still optimal, and you can't have them if you invested in residential properties.

More Flexible Lease Terms

With commercial leases, there are fewer consumer protection laws to be observed. Contrary to residential real estate, you will have to squeeze yourself in and submit to many state laws that include termination rules and security deposit limits.

NEGATIVE POINTS FOR COMMERCIAL PROPERTY INVESTING

Though you will find many positive indications for you to start investing in the commercial real estate world, still, there are some disadvantages that you would have to look at also.

Time Commitment

If your property investment is a commercial retail building with a few or more tenants, you still have more work to do when it comes to property management than with a residential investment. If you want to maximize your investment return, you can't be an absentee lessor. You have to deal with multiple leases, more maintenance issues, public safety concerns, and annual CAM (Common Area Maintenance) cost adjustments that your renters should shoulder. In short, you have more in your hands, and you also have to make your property look impressive in the public eye, same as with your tenants.

Professional Help Required

Commercial property maintenance issues will require professionals to take over if you are not licensed to handle the maintenance work single-handedly. So, expect and prepare for an additional set of expenses as you will probably hire those who will come to your aid during emergencies and property repairs so that everything will be kept in top shape.

Also, consider the property management expenses when you evaluate the asking price for your commercial property investment. You could charge between 5-10% of the rent revenues for property management services with the inclusion of lease administration. Assess yourself if you can or want to manage the leasing and the relationships. If not, you could outsource the responsibilities.

Bigger Initial Investment

Although you can find residential and commercial properties within the same area, you will realize that you will need more capital to acquire commercial properties than residential properties. That's one reason why most investors find it more challenging to invest in commercial real estate.

Not only that, it's typical that large capital expenditures will follow after you procured your commercial property. After a few months, you could have a $10,000 bill you acquired from roofing repairs or make a new furnace. More customers mean more facility maintenance and costs. Therefore, you'll need (and hope for) your revenue gains to outweigh your expenses to support your commercial investment.

More Risks to Deal With

Since commercial properties are for the use of public visitors, your property will most likely be prone to damage as more people visit your place. Cars may hit your patrons in the parking lot, people can slip on ice in winter, and your building could get spray paint from vandals.

Though such incidents do happen almost everywhere, commercial properties are more at risk for these happenings. In case you'd prefer not to handle too risky investments, consider investing in residential properties.

TYPES OF COMMERCIAL PROPERTIES

Commercial Properties can be are categorized into five different types, which are:

Retail

Retail Building is a popular commercial real estate type consisting of community retail centers, restaurants, banks, and strip malls located in urban areas. The size of these properties ranges from 5,000 to 350,000 square feet.

Offices

Office space is the most common commercial real estate property type. These buildings, which range from single rentable offices up to skyscrapers, are classified into three different categories:

Class A

Class A Commercial Properties are newly-built or renovated buildings located in primary areas with easy access to amenities such as food, medicine, and fuel. In short, they are the best buildings in terms of location, aesthetics, quality of infrastructure, and age. These buildings are usually managed by professional real estate management companies.

Class B

Class B Commercial Properties are older buildings usually targeted for restoration and that require capital investment. They may be well-managed but still require upgrades and minor repairs, making them a good investment in real estate.

Class C

Class C commercial Properties are the oldest properties used for development opportunities, usually located in poor strategic areas requiring huge capital investments to improve infrastructure. Their high vacancy rates are much higher than high-class buildings because of their poor locations.

Multifamily Properties

Multifamily properties are composed of high-rise condominiums, apartment complexes, and small multifamily units or houses. The property is automatically qualified as multifamily real estate when it has more than one unit but can also be considered commercial when it has four or more units.

Many residential investors build their real estate investment portfolio by starting in commercial properties before expanding into larger multifamily properties. Tenant turnover is also a factor that needs consideration since residential tenants tend to have shorter lease terms compared to office and retail tenants.

Industrial Commercial Buildings

Industrial, commercial buildings such as warehouses are geared towards manufacturing industries, offering spaces with height specifications and docking availability. Commercial properties lend more to investment opportunities.

Special Purpose

Special Purpose buildings are designed for specific use in a way that it is difficult to repurpose for different use.

Examples of these are car washes, schools, and self-storage facilities. Tourism and leisure industries can be considered as special purpose facilities as well. Such facilities include hotels, airports, stadiums, and amusement parks.

Mixed or Multiple

Development properties are also in demand in the commercial real estate sector. These properties are composed of two or more facilities with different purposes or uses, such as the retail, public, and residential sector. Such buildings can have shopping and service facilities on the first floor and apartment units on other floors.

PROS AND CONS OF COMMERCIAL REAL ESTATE INVESTING

Commercial Real Estate Investing can be very rewarding in terms of financial and personal reasons. Most people invest in it for passive income and security, while others utilize it for tax benefits and diversification of their investment portfolio.

COMMERCIAL REAL ESTATE INVESTING BENEFITS

Listed below are other benefits that a redeveloper can benefit from commercial real estate investing:

Business Relationship

Commercial Real Estate offers its investors the opportunity to participate in business-to-business relationships. It leads to more professional and neighbourly interactions with your tenants compared to residential ones. You may even be able to build and establish business relationships with business owners renting your property. It can expand your network and get involved in the community you are investing your money in.

Less Competition

There is less competition in commercial real estate compared to residential ones. Because of its difficulty, the business network here is saturated and only available to higher capital investment.

Longer Leases

One of the biggest perks in commercial real estate investing is the duration of leasing contracts. Compared to residential real estate, commercial real estate properties have a longer lease time, making them less likely to vacancy. In most cases, tenants lease commercial property for a minimum of one decade.

Limited Operational Hours

This perk may be less known, but, for the most part, commercial real estate investors share working hours with their tenants, which means lesser time for maintenance requests, communication with tenants, utility consumption, etc. Unlike in residential areas where someone is needed to be available 24/7 for tenants, commercial property owners can limit it to a work hour window. In other words, any unresolved issue will be deal with on the next working day.

Higher Income Potentials

Higher potential income is the main reason behind commercial real estate investing. In general, commercial properties have more significant and higher investment returns compared to single-family properties. Next, commercial properties have a lower vacancy risk since they tend to have more available units.

Consistent Cash Flow

Commercial real estate properties have a consistent stream of income due to their more extended lease periods than residential properties. Commercial properties have more units, making it possible to increase income streams more quickly. Commercial Real Estate Investing can be very rewarding in terms of financial and personal reasons. Most people invest in it for passive income and security, while others utilize it for tax benefits and diversification of their investment portfolio.

THE DOWNSIDES OF INVESTING IN COMMERCIAL PROPERTY

Commercial Real Estate Investing can be very rewarding in terms of financial and personal reasons. Most people invest in it for passive income and security, while others utilize it for tax benefits and diversification of their investment portfolio.

Listed below are other benefits that a redeveloper can benefit from commercial real estate investing:

Business Relationship

Commercial Real Estate offers its investors the opportunity to participate in business-to-business relationships. It leads to more professional and neighbourly interactions with your tenants compared to residential ones. You may even be able to build and establish business relationships with business owners renting your property. It can expand your network and get involved in the community you are investing your money in.

Less Competition

Commercial property rentals are less competitive compared to residential rentals due to the saturated business network higher capital investment.

Longer Leases

One of the biggest perks in commercial real estate investing is the duration of leasing contracts. Compared to residential real estate, commercial real estate properties have a longer lease time, making them less likely to vacancy. In most cases, tenants lease commercial property for a minimum of one decade.

Limited Operational Hours

This perk may be less known, but, for the most part, commercial real estate investors share working hours with their tenants, which means lesser time for maintenance requests, communication with tenants, utility consumption, etc. Unlike in residential areas where someone is needed to be available 24/7 for tenants, commercial property owners can limit it to a work hour window. In other words, any unresolved issue will be deal with on the next working day.

Higher Income Potential

Higher potential income is the main reason behind commercial real estate investing. In general, commercial properties have more significant and higher investment returns compared to single-family properties. Next, commercial properties have a lower vacancy risk since they tend to have more available units.

Consistent Cash Flow

Commercial real estate properties have a consistent stream of income due to their more extended lease periods than residential properties. Commercial properties have more units, making it possible to increase income streams more quickly. Commercial Real Estate Investing can be very rewarding in terms of financial and personal reasons. Most people invest in it for passive income and security, while others utilize it for tax benefits and diversification of their investment portfolio.

THINGS YOU NEED TO KNOW BEFORE INVESTING

Commercial Real Estate is a lucrative and appealing investment due to its consistent returns, growth potential, and passive income. While CRE has excellent profit potential, but not all are equal. Having a clear understanding of the "what, when, and how" to invest in commercial real estate can help you determine its success your failure. Having enough knowledge is an essential component of successful investing to help you avoid common mistakes, pitfalls, and risks and prepare you before acquiring the property.

NOT ALL PROPERTY TYPES ARE THE SAME

If you decide to invest in commercial real estate, here are the things that you need to know.

Not All Property Types are the Same

Commercial real estate is classified into five main sectors, namely;

- Industrial

- Multifamily

- Office

- Retail

- Special Purposes

However, there are many other property types such as hotel, self-storage, land, elder care, etc. Each sector varies significantly in terms of demand, returns, and overall profitability.

Some property types perform better than others based on supply and demand in certain areas. It is essential to develop the skill to identify the asset types that are most profitable or offer enormous opportunities.

Before investing, research how each asset performs in the current economy and determine the viability of that sector as an investment. Only then can you choose the property type that you intend to pursue.

Know the Market

Another thing that is different in the investing sector is the market. When investing, you are investing in a specific geographical location with its unique supply and demand. Certain property types could be doing well on the macro level, but the market may move the opposite way when there is oversupply in your local area. Conducting thorough market research can help you determine if there is a potential market risk of market saturation.

Understand Market Cycles

The profitability of commercial real estate is always affected by the economy's health, GDP, and employment rate. Therefore you must understand how real estate market cycles work and how they can help you avoid buying when the market is high and selling when it is low. Furthermore, knowing specific metrics of the different market cycles will help determine what opportunities are currently present to make informed investment decisions.

Do Thorough Diligence

Conducting thorough research on every investment opportunity is necessary when investing. It includes reviewing financial statements, tax returns, and other information necessary in evaluating or assessing the profitability of a property which you to acquire.

New investors often get too excited at the prospect of buying a property that they miss conducting their due diligence thoroughly. Knowing what needs to be examined, investigated, and analyzed before making a deal will save you from potential mistakes that can be very costly. Because of some economic factors, market cycles, or challenges that may occur after investing in the property, its performance can fluctuate, affecting your return and profitability. It's ultimately the fund manager's job to inform you of this risk properly, but it's also good to be conscious of it on your own.

Maintain a Contingency and Capital Reserve Fund

Uncertainty is an element of any investment that, regardless of how you do your due diligence, there are always unexpected factors that may arise. Such factors may positively or negatively affect the performance of your investment. To hedge this uncertainty is to have a contingency fund that will cushion any e impact on your investment.

As part of your initial acquisition cost, set aside cost contingencies to spend when unexpected expenses arise like rezoning, immediate renovation, change management, etc.

The standard contingency budget in commercial real estate is 5-15%. However, it can vary depending on the asset and its performance. Cost contingencies are helpful when you incur negative cash flow while improving the property's overall performance.

Additionally, creating a capital reserve fund is one best practice in commercial real estate. It is a fund account that you should set aside for long-term improvements (Frankel, 2021). Generally, it is 3-5% of your annual gross revenue (Hananel, 2013).

Anticipate Setbacks and Extended Timelines

While there are uncertainties with cost, there is also uncertainty in time. Most investors, especially beginners, set unrealistic timelines for building, renovating, and many other related CRE investments. Expect some setbacks and challenges to occur anytime, which can stall the progress of your investment. Try to anticipate potential obstacles so you can prepare before it even happens.

HOW TO GET STARTED

To get started in commercial rental property investing, here are the steps that you need to follow to avoid losses in the rental estate arena.

STEP #1 - MIND YOUR DUE DILIGENCE

Master the Property Location

You must know the area well. Know if there are demands for commercial rental property and the prevailing rules and laws in real estate. You must be familiar with the local market before taking a step further. Only do so after checking on the market – demand, competition, regional trends, etc.

Do Research on the Property

It is essential to gather information about your target property to get a good deal.

Understand the Seller

Know the Deal

Due diligence lets you decide if the deal is worth pursuing. Through research you have conducted, you will have a higher chance of acquiring the property successfully.

STEP #2 - BUILD UP YOUR CREDIBILITY

Create a template that you can use in looking for property sellers. This template can be personalized to each seller and must include the following:

- Contact info

- Business description

- Core business services

A personalized template will make the lender feel important and make them see you as a professional

STEP #3 - FIND A PROPERTY

You can find properties via the following

- Direct mail

- Networking

- Craigslist

- Bandit signs

- MLS

Keep updated on local commercial real estate networking events in your area.

STEP #4 - PREPARE YOUR FINANCES

Always keep your financial records ready to show potential lenders. Some significant calculations to include are:

- Loan to Value Ratio – measures value of the loan vs. the value of property

- Debt Service Coverage – measures the ability of the property to service a debt

- Creditworthiness – measures how likely the borrower is to default on their loan.

Make sure to separate your investment credit from personal credit by creating an LLC for your business. It will somehow protect you and your business.

STEP # 5 - CREATE A LONG-TERM PLAN

- Hire a property manager

- Hire a maintenance staff

Ask referrals from your local network. Shortlist potential candidates/companies and conduct interviews to make sure if they are a good fit.

CALCULATING COMMERCIAL PROPERTY INVESTMENT RETURNS

The goal of any investor is to gain profit. So if you are investing in rental property, it is because you want to earn money. The more significant investment you have, the bigger profit you expect to return to you out of that investment.

One thing that attracts people to commercial real estate is the monthly cash flow and the opportunity for property appreciation. But how would you know if your investment is doing well?

To know, you must be able to calculate the commercial real estate investment returns.

Cash on Cash or Return on investment (ROI)

Also called the Rate of Return (ROR), the Return on Investment (ROI) indicates the increase or decrease in an investment over a set period (Banton, 2020).

The Return on Investment (ROI) or simply cash on cash is the most common investment metric used in all real estate.

It is calculated by getting the annual cash flow of a property asset and divides it by the total amount you invested in the property.

Formula of ROI

$$\mathbf{ROI} = \frac{\text{CASH FLOW}}{\text{DOWN PAYMENT}}$$

To illustrate:

Cash flow = $2,000   Down Payment = $200,000

ROI = $2,000/$200,000 = 10%

Benefits of Return on Investment

It provides you with a quick view of the investment profitability, which you can compare to the stock market investment or other investment vehicles.

Because it is cash-based, it is an excellent way to determine returns.

Drawbacks of Cash on Cash

While being simple, it can also be a drawback. ROI only provides you with a measurement of return based on your initial investment at a given time. It does not consider the value of money, nor does it measure your return based on a capital build-up on the property.

Internal Rate of Return (IRR)

Financial analysts and investors use the Internal Rate of Return as a metric to estimate the profitability of potential investments and to see if the investment is justifiable. It is a discount rate that makes the Net Present Value (NPV) of all cash flows in a discounted cash flow analysis equal to zero. The use of IRR when obtaining the present net worth in financial analysis is known as the discounted cash flow method.

The IRR Rule is an essential guideline when making a decision on whether to proceed with the investment project or abandon the idea completely.

The measurement of IRR is high-level. To calculate your IRR, you consider your initial investment, distribution of cash flow, and the duration of the investment.

The Formula for the Internal Rate of Return

One algebraic formula that you may use to calculate IRR is:

$$\textbf{IRR} = R1 + (NPV1 \times (R2 - R1) (NVP1 - NVP2)$$

R1, R2 (discount selected at random)

NPV1 (Higher Net Present Value)

NPV2 (Lower Net Present Value)

Factors that are significant here are:

- Amount of investment

- Timing of the total investment

- Associated cash flow from the investment

Some complicated formulas are necessary for distinguishing between periods of net cash inflow.

The initial step is to make your guesses for the possible values of R1 and R2. Your guesses will help you determine the NVPs (Net Present Value). Experienced investors have developed the sense to make fair guesses.

If the estimated NVP1 is near zero, the IRR is equal to R1. You have to understand that the entire equation is set up based on the knowledge that at the IRR, NPV is equal to zero. There are other ways to calculate IRR, but you have to follow the process. If the NPV is too far from zero, then try again by making another guess.

The purpose for calculating IRR includes

- Mortgage analysis

- Private equity investments

- Lending decisions

Understand that IRR models do not include the cost of capital and assume that all cash inflows earned within the life of the project are reinvested back at the same rate as IRR.

IRR accounts for the length of time that you invest your money. So, while the Cash on Cash Return helps determine the initial quality of an investment, it is only but a snapshot and frozen in time.

When you use IRR, you can compare the different lengths of investments and their potential returns, so you will know which direction is best suited for you.

However, using IRR also has its definite drawbacks. For one, it is too complicated to calculate, and it is not a measurement that you can efficiently perform in your mind while just seeing your prospective investment. You have to use a spreadsheet for it. It also takes into account variables like future cash flows and estimated sales costs.

RETURN ON EQUITY = NET INCOME/EQUITY

This measurement of investment is not so popular but should be on top of the list of every sophisticated investor.

The Return on Equity considers your total capital built over time and measures your cash returns against your total equity and not only on your investment.

Your Return on Equity will show you if your equity is not giving you back enough return to call your investment profitable. At some point, you will cross a threshold where your returns are lower than your capital build-up. You will know when to pull out your investment and divert it to other projects through your ROI.

While ROE is an excellent measurement for financial analysis of investment, remember that your capital here is on the property. To realize your return, you have to refinance or take out a line of credit.

Seasoned investors are using all these three financial tools to maximize their potential investment returns. You might as well learn all these three if you want to do what they are doing.

MARKETING COMMERCIAL PROPERTIES

There are many routes to take and strategies to initiate when it comes to commercial real estate marketing. Listing platforms, Chamber of Commerce meetings, Networking Events, and Social Media are only a few of those. However, these solid strategies only work best depending on the category and the type of audience. Successful marketing, after all, is all about catering to the needs of your target audience, reaching them at the right place at the right time with just the right message.

MULTIFAMILY COMMERCIAL REAL ESTATE MARKETING

Because of the pandemic, most multifamily tenants will prefer finding you online, so you have to increase your online presence and virtually deliver the feel, look, and ambience of your development. It means you should:

- Increase your social presence, using your tenants as social influencers and probably advertisers

- Create 3D, virtual, or augmented reality-experience tours that will allow potential tenants to explore your community from anywhere

- Invest in high-quality photos and videos

- Create and optimize your website for Search Engine Optimization (SEO), mainly focusing on phrases and frequently-used keywords.

- List your units on multiple online platforms like Zillow, Zumper, or Apartments.com.

- Creating or offering incentives like free rent for the month, waived application fees, free movers, and more can persuade your tenants to step up. Partner up with organizations in your community and show them your brand. That way, you get to advertise yourself as well.

RETAIL PROPERTY MARKETING

If you have retail properties, your current tenants can help you market those. If you own small shopping centers and strip malls, your visibility grows as your tenants or retailers progress over time. It helps to promote your clients and your business, and here are some of the most valuable ideas:

- Creating a search-optimized website with a detailed list of your partner retailers and shops

- Hosting events such as market days during holidays and other occasions

- Getting your properties mentioned in social media or local press to raise brand awareness

- Utilizing social media marketing by tagging your partners and retailers in photos, sharing their posts, and reposting content from clients and customers

By increasing the business of your clients, you are also increasing the traffic to your property. Additionally, by supporting your potential tenants, you are also helping them grow their business. And by also asking your client for referrals and advertising in trade magazines and search engines, you are solidifying your brand.

OFFICE BUILDING MARKETING

When it comes to office buildings, you may need to use a more business-like approach. Besides SEO and advertising, you may also list your properties on commercial real estate platforms like LoopNet, CREXi, Ten-X, etc. You can also try the methods below:

- Join your area's Chamber of Commerce

- Join networking events with executives and business leaders can also be done virtually due to the pandemic. Advertise via newspapers, magazines, and classified sections

- Invest in quality advertisements outside your building or key roads near you

With many businesses struggling due to pandemic-related shutdowns, offering incentives will be a great help to them. You can also install antimicrobial LED lights, air purifiers, and other sanitary facilities and equipment to ensure their employees' safety while working.

INDUSTRIAL SPACE REAL ESTATE MARKETING

Advertising through trade magazines is an excellent platform for promoting industrial buildings. If you have buildings made for a specific purpose, e.g., warehouses, data centers, factories, or cold storage, find publications in that particular industry and create an occasional ad. You may post advertisements on the website of these publications. You can also do these things below:

- Take drone photos of the entire facility and posting them on your website, social media, Vimeo, or Google.

- Join the Chamber of Commerce

- Host a broker event to get into the local real estate community.

- Create a search-engine-optimized website that breaks down your building's features, location, benefits, etc.

You can also use commercial property databases such as CBRE, CREXI, and LoopNet to advertise your property.

COMMERCIAL REAL ESTATE LOAN TYPES

Now that you have enough knowledge of commercial real estate investing, including its startup ideas and its benefits, an important aspect should now be considered. That is, how will you finance those investments?

There are many commercial investment loan types, and it is up to investors to decide which type of financing will suit their needs. Each loan type has a unique eligibility requirement such as experience level, credit score, and down payment. These loans also have payment terms, which usually include interest rate, loan term, and the loan-to-value ratio. One investor may search for a loan that offers low interest but has a longer payment term compared to the rest, while others prioritize finding a short-term loan to bridge a present financial gap.

Listed below are the different types of commercial real estate loans:

- Conventional Loan

- Hard Money Loan

- Certified Development Company (CDC)/SBA 504 Loan

- Small Business Administration 7(a) Loan

- Commercial Bridge Loan

- Conduit Loan

GETTING A COMMERCIAL REAL ESTATE LOAN

At first, it may seem intimidating, if not daring, to try obtaining commercial real estate financing. However, investors who know the process as well as the different commercial real estate loan types find it attainable.

Listed below are the steps to obtain a commercial investment property loan:

Mortgage Options

Investors must realize that commercial and residential mortgages are not the same. Unlike residential mortgages, commercial mortgages are not government-supported. Additionally, commercial loans range from five to twenty years, while residential ones usually range from fifteen to thirty years. Lenders will also make their decisions based on the investor's financial and credit history.

Debt Service Coverage Ratio

Moneylenders also tend to look at debt-service coverage ratio (DSCR), which measures a property's ability to service debt. This compares a property's annual net operating income to its annual mortgage debt service, which also includes the principal and interest. A DSR of one percent or less means negative cash flow, while a 1.25% DSCR is recommended to ensure a property's cash flow.

Individuality vs. Reality

One should determine whether to finance a commercial property as an entity or an individual. Most commercial real estate properties nowadays are purchased by developers, corporations, and business partnerships. The lender makes certain that the borrower can repay the loan, hence requiring the borrower to provide financial track records to secure the loan. They will also require the investor to guarantee the loan for new businesses with no credit history.

Loan to Value Ratio

Lenders consider a property's loan-to-value (LTV) ratio as an important metric when financing commercial real estate. This figure determines the value of the loan against the value of the property itself. It is done by dividing the loan amount by the property's purchase price or appraisal value. The LTV required for commercial loans usually ranges from sixty-five to eighty percent, while lower LTVs qualify for more favourable financing rates.

Once you have secured your commercial property investment's financing, you are now prepared to search through various financial listings. However, this much information is hard to process all at once, so it is advised to keep reading. That way, you will have your most urgent questions answered from time to time.

SINGLE FAMILY/CONDOMINIUM UNITS

UNDERSTANDING SINGLE FAMILY HOMES AND CONDOMINIUM UNITS

A single-family home is an independent residential structure designed for use as a single dwelling unit with one kitchen and unshared walls and utilities. It sits on a parcel of land. However, if you want a broader definition, let us consider the description given by the U.S. Census Bureau (Wikipedia contributors, 2020). A single-family house may be fully detached – a row house or a townhouse. Still, it must be separated from the adjacent unit by a ground-to-roof wall to be considered a single-family home for one that is attached to other homes. Also, units attached in some way to another must not share heating or air-conditioning systems or utilities or have other housing units located above or below.

Single-family rental housing tends to have higher "tenant stickiness" - e.g., tenants are less likely inclined to move as often due to the following reasons:

Privacy

Most tenants prefer to live a few distances away from their neighbours. It's not peaceful to hear the sounds of other tenants arguing through a thin wall or kids running nonstop on the unit just above yours.

More Space

Single-family homes offer more space which diminishes the tendency to feel claustrophobic.

Provides Emotional Attachment

Single-family living provides an emotional attachment to the property, offering more chances for long-term settlement on your rental property. Indeed tenants love to plant flowers they love, add patio furniture, and watch their kids play in the front yard.

For them, it becomes their home and not just a place to rent.

Available Free On-Site Storage

Americans love hoarding stuff and a single-family property provides more storage space than other types of housing – attics, sheds, closets, and basements.

Feels More Like Home

When there is a larger space inside and outside, like patio or yard, tenants with pets and children find themselves comfortable and tend to become more permanently set up in a single-family property. See how they enjoy seeing their kids and dogs romp and play in a property secured by a fence.

School Stability

Single-family homes are attractive for families with children enrolled in schools they love, and changing schools often because of changing residence can be disruptive for parents and their kids. It is avoidable if the family feels settled in your property.

Other Conveniences

Single-family homes provide conveniences and amenities not often present in other rental options, including off-street parking or garage parking, washer and dryer, and additional living space.

SINGLE FAMILY HOMES VS. CONDOMINIUM UNITS

People, who want to have their residence end up with two basic choices when it comes to residential estate purchases: would it be a house or a condo?

Both types of real estate residences have their own set of advantages and disadvantages. Nevertheless, the living experience for each type of residence differs significantly from the other.

For those who have families, a single-family home is a classic preference, while for the first time and older purchasers, condominiums have a distinctive appeal for them.

Still, before you decide to purchase a rental property, as a wise investor, you should at least be knowledgeable about the basic differences between a house and a condo.

In this chapter, the pros and cons of a house and a condominium would be explored. It could offer you some light to both types of residence so that you could choose which would suit the taste and needs of your target market.

PROS AND CONS OF CONDOS AND HOMES

Size

Mostly, condominiums are limited when it comes to size, unlike houses. But there are still exemptions because you can find numerous two-bedroom houses that have fewer floor/ lot areas than large condos.

Since condos are designed and built, going upward (height) and not outward (expanse), expect them to be smaller than most houses. And if space is concerned, it's not a disadvantage.

Smaller living spaces may be ideal for you, depending on what you need for your home. If your living space is smaller, you will have less area for cleaning and also less for accumulating clutter.

But then, condominium buyers have something to consider and understand with condos. Oftentimes, condominiums have certain restrictions that will prohibit tenants from creating another bedroom.

For instance, there's an unfinished basement. You might think of renovating it so that it could turn into another bedroom. Though you can renovate it to become another bedroom, if the time comes that you want to sell it, you can't market your condo as you have renovated it.

Maintenance

This aspect is considered to be a plus point for buying condos. Property owners, especially older ones, who no longer feel that they could keep up a landscape or yard, choose condos because of these maintenance issues.

External maintenance involving several tasks includes lawn mowing, weeding flower beds, and keeping plants in your possession alive. Aside from that, you will also take tons of leaves during fall, depending on what part of the country you are in.

You may find some people who enjoy doing the external maintenance while others prefer to pay the costs of professional fees to have the work done. So, if you are looking at buying a condo, asking questions with regards to external maintenance is vital.

You should ask about what would be the exact coverage of the condo fees and what you would be responsible for when you become a property owner. Probably, these would be the answers that you could get for that question:

Your fees would cover the association's upkeep of the grounds shared with all other owners. Mostly, the landscape is designed to minimize maintenance.

You will pay for your unit's maintenance. However, you also share the upkeep cost for everything communal (e.g. the roof of the condo).

But if you are going to sum up all the maintenance costs of a condo versus a house, it would be typically less than what it would cost you for a house's upkeep.

Privacy

If you value your privacy much, a house would be a better option for you since houses are commonly separated from the other by at least a small area of land. On the contrary, with a condo, you share spaces with all other condo owners. This is mostly a major difference where house buyers look at and tends to form a big part in their decision-making.

As for condominiums, though privacy becomes a trade-off with condos, you could access and share common areas with other condominium owners. Amenities like a sauna, pool, fitness center, or hot tub are just examples of what condo owners share and the others that would surely cost you a very hefty amount of cash if you buy for yourself. Also, sharing these common areas with your neighbours could bring you closer to them.

Financial Health

This is another area where a huge difference between houses and condos is easily seen.

With condominiums, an association is in charge when it comes to the management of the neighbourhood's financial health. Here, the owners are required to pay a monthly or quarterly fee that would serve as their contribution for necessities such as trash and snow removal, insurance, landscaping, overall maintenance, etc.

On the contrary, a standalone house that doesn't have anything to do with homeowners' associations does not hold any of these considerations. Your own house is fully at your disposal, and you won't have worries about neighbours who may be delinquent in paying their fees.

Financing in General

Finding finances (mortgage) for purchasing a house or a condo also differs from one another.

Let's say you decided on purchasing a house. Essentially, you just get the type of mortgage that you want, and that's it. Select the loan type (FHA, VA, or conventional) as long as you qualify for it.

However, you should verify what type of loan you could be able to use when you decide to purchase a condo. For example, there are condo developments that don't have FHA approval. You ask yourself why they are not after FHA approval. It won't cost them a lot of money to get FHA approved. Yet, such condo associations disregard this because they simply don't get why it's important.

But this is a great advantage for condo buyers. When you are qualified for getting an FHA loan, you would only have to come up with 3.5% as your down payment to your advantage.

Now, if you are interested in getting a condo, be sure to ask your realtor straight away whether the condo is FHA approved in case you are planning to use FHA as your way of finance. Why? So that you wouldn't have much problem in financing your condo purchase and the long-term value of your property won't be affected. Most buyers are locked out of purchasing a condo unit when the condo development is not approved by FHA.

Location

Another area that may be an advantage for having a condominium is its location (though it still depends on your priorities if it is an advantage for you). Since a condominium takes less land perimeter than houses, they are often located in cities or at least much closer to cities where most people want to dwell. The resurgence of living in urban places has made condos popular lately.

As for full-size houses, you will find them to be less likely found in the center of cities. If ever you see them, expect them to cost you a fortune. So, if you still want to own a home in a city, condos may only be the affordable option you could get. Though you'll have limited space compared to what you'll have in a house, this could be a very reasonable option in exchange for all the perks you can access in the location.

Control

There are certain arrangements where buyers of residential properties get involved as they purchase a particular property. You could purchase a house that you are free to do whatsoever you wish to do with it. There is also an instance wherein you become a part of a homeowners association (HOA) upon purchase of a house in a certain neighbourhood. Also, upon buying a condo unit (as the case with most condominiums), there is a community organization that oversees the maintenance of each unit in the complex. May it be a house in a neighbourhood or a condo unit, being fully familiar with the advantages and disadvantages of an HOA is crucial.

If you want major control of your home, buying a single-family house that has no HOA ties would be the best for you.

You wouldn't be forced to comply with any of the standards, rules, or safety nets that an HOA sets and maintains within their area. You can do whatever you want with your house as long as you don't obstruct any rule that is set by the county you are in.

If you decide to purchase a house with an HOA, expect that you won't have that much freedom as with those residents without an HOA in their neighbourhood. You need to observe the rules that are set, which mostly deals with what you can only do to the exterior part of your home, such as the number of vehicles you could only park in the driveway or if you could park on the street. Such rules, upon compliance, provide your neighbourhood with a particular quality standard.

As for purchasing a condo, you will find yourself in a position that is almost the same as those who have homes with HOAs. Aside from the necessary rules that you need to observe, there is also the membership due. An organization would see to it that everything is under control.

Not only the same roof and other common areas are being shared by the condo homeowners, but you all also share financial responsibility regarding the complex.

Associations could be a good or bad thing; it depends on the people who are in the position. But then, if you reside in a place where there are rules that give you discomfort, it can make your life miserable. Thus, do some research first about the association where you plan to purchase your residence – that is, if they are good at running things or not. You could ask and get the opinions of those who are already residing in the area. You could also ask a local realtor, and they will know if that particular neighbourhood has an unruly HOA.

Cost

When it comes to costing, single-family houses would cost you more than what condominiums cost. This is because of the privileges discussed on the above aspects and what you will get when you purchase a house for your residence:

- Control

- Privacy

- More space

But if you want a more affordable option, you are already retiring, and you want to stretch your finances and/or limit your external maintenance, condos could be a better match for you. One of the main advantages of purchasing a condo is the cost, aside from any other reasons you might have for buying one.

Now, it's your decision which of the two would suit your current lifestyle. As long as your decision reflects sense from your financial and emotional standpoint, you could enjoy your residential property purchase.

DEVELOPING A GAME PLAN

Developing a game plan is crucial to an investor. Using a lousy strategy or badly applying it may cause a deal to fall apart, and worse, you can lose money.

There are two levels at which you can apply a strategy – high level and low level. Sometimes these two levels overlap.

On the high level, you may think of a strategy that will help you build wealth through the rental property like:

- Purchasing undervalued property and renovating it

- Develop new homes from scratch and have them rented

- Seek repossessed properties

- Specialized in Multiple-family rental or Airbnb

- Buy multiple high-yield properties and rent them out

- Use creative strategies to avoid investing any of your own money.

Typically, it is best to pick one property investment strategy and master it or combine any of the above strategies that complement each other.

If you are new to the rental investing trade, you should have hands-on training to gain experience instead of hiring someone to do the job for you. It's only reasonable to hire a property manager when you already acquire enough knowledge of rental property investing along with its ins and outs. This way, you can still have control over your business by keeping track of activities via reports and checking them from time to time. It can be dangerous to get into the rental business when you don't know anything about it and rely on other people to manage it.

Once you have master one vesting option like single-family home rental and become successful, you may move on to adding more single-family homes. You may also try buying multiple-families rental property or commercial companies when your investment funds allow you.

It would be best to create a game plan before diving deep into investing so you won't want time, money, and energy. Without a definite game plan, you are likely to change your mind every time you find a new opportunity that you think is a good one. However, you have to remember that Jack of all trade is a master of none and if you don't want to end up with anything worth regretting- having skills and experience can be more valuable than money. You can always start all over again, and this time, more sure of yourself and your success.

When one moment you are thinking of buying off a property, and the next minute, you are thinking about a straightforward buy-to-let investing. Your business will only start to take off when you decide to stick to one investment option and master it.

CHOOSING THE BEST STRATEGY

When planning, here are some of the things that you need to consider.

PERSONALITY

What type of person are you. Are you the sociable type who loves meeting people? IF you are the introvert type, then you are most likely to partner with someone who knows how to negotiate as this is all about dealing with various types of people.

- What skills do you have?

- Are you a handyman?

- Do you have good communication skills?

- Do you have administrative skills

- Are you good at creating content?

- Are you good at marketing or advertising?

- Do you have knowledge of information technology?

- Do you have influencing skills that can motivate people to follow you?

You can use any or all of these skills to your advantage. For example, if you have a background in Information Technology, you can develop websites and create online marketing campaigns to help you find your tenants.

If you have the ability to negotiate, then you could be good at selling and influencing people. Put this to use, and you will bring in more good tenants to make your rental property investing a great success.

TIME

Time is vital in any business, and so it is in rental property investing. It would help if you had time to find the best property, negotiate for the best deal, gather information about the target property, look for funds to finance the property, and handle the administrative part of the whole business operation. More than everything, you need time to learn whatever knowledge you need to acquire to be in the game.

Time is a valuable commodity. If you don't have time, you have to pay someone to do what you can't do because you don't have it. However, this can mean losing money and the opportunity to learn something out of what you could have done.

WHAT IS YOUR RISK-TOLERANCE?

Not all businesses end up successfully. In the world of investing, the higher the risk, the bigger the profit. The real estate business is meant for the long-term, but you need the highest level of risk tolerance if you want to gain profit out of your investment.

Of all investment assets, land proves to be one asset class that does not depreciate or loses its value which makes it tolerant to inflation and because investing in rental property involves investing in the land and the structure that comes with it, there is a great possibility that you will incur losses if your cash flow is consistently below your expenses.

However, remember that the structure is only a part of the whole property and the value of the land where your property sits never goes down, so you will never incur a loss on your total investment unless you sell it at a price below its purchase amount. As long as you hold on to the land, you will still gain profit through appreciation.

LOCATION

Many investors invest in properties remote to their base. However, it is best to concentrate on your local area that suits well to your property investment strategy. For example, if you live in a tourist belt, then Airbnb is definitely a good choice for

Although it is tempting to find a property across the country once opportunities are presented, it can become very difficult to manage.

INVESTMENT GOAL

If your investment goal is to have a consistent cash flow, rental property is then suitable for you, especially multi-family rentals where you can have a monthly cash flow as long as your property units are occupied.

THE PROPERTY MARKET

The choice of rental property strategy can also be determined by the prevailing market.

WHAT ABOUT LOW-LEVEL STRATEGY?

This is the kind of strategy that an investor employs for a specific transaction or deal. It can be conventional like the usual buy-to-let you can get more creative in your property investment strategies like lease options.

Examples of low-level strategies are:

- Buying properties at auction

- Lease Options

- Add value and refinance

Before committing to any deal, decide the strategy you will use.

CHAPTER 3: THE STRATEGY

Once you pursue real estate education, you will eventually encounter the

BRRRR word. And whenever you listen to an expert real estate investor's advice, you will also hear of it one way or another. However, it doesn't mean that they are feeling cold. Instead, it is an acronym that stands for **Buy**, **Rehab**, **Rent**, **Refinance**, and **Repeat**. In other words, the acronym stands for a real estate investor's business investment cycle.

> *"Risk comes from not knowing what you're doing."* - *Warren Buffett*

The usual method of acquiring rental property by real estate investors involves buying the desired property through financing such as a mortgage, then rehab it, have it rented, and repeating the strategy over again. It's a convenient and popular method since you can purchase properties through a loan, which usually comes from a bank. After securing the down payment, which is around 20-25%, the investor doesn't have to work too hard just to save up the property's full purchase price, making the method an ideal move for every smart investor.

BUY

In real estate, you are making money when you buy a property. You do this by purchasing properties below their market value and never investing more than 70% of your property ARV or After Repair Value of the property.

In calculating the ARV for your property, you need to have a conservative estimate of the appraised value of the property after repairing it. Take that figure and multiply it by 70%. Your goal as an investor is to make the cost of repairing your home, and the amount you use to buy your home adds up to your ARV. Other investors opt for 75%. However, this can be too tight for budget adjustments, especially when you include financing cost, vacancies, plus the possibility that you may fall short of your appraisal value expectation.

A good tactic is to purchase homes that need significant repairs because other buyers are less likely to want to invest in this type of property, and you can also negotiate the price down. Here are good examples of affordable repairs that can increase the value of your property because you manage to get a good deal.

Damages Drywalls: Damaged drywalls deter financing investors and can cause the property's ineligibility for financing. Fixing drywalls won't break the bank, so fid those damages before they can harm your credit financing.

Deteriorating Kitchens:

No investor will appreciate a kitchen that appears to be more of a ruin. Try giving your kitchen a new look, and you are more likely to impress the inspector.

Roofs: A leaky roof will surely bring your property appraisal value. Make a few fixes or replace your old roofing with a new one to get a better appraisal property.

Bad Landscaping: A good landscape can impress anyone who visits your property, including a financing inspector. Plant a few hedges and create a mini garden to create a cool ambiance in front and around your property. A splash of colours is sure to bring life to it and entice potential renters.

Outdated Bathrooms: Since bathrooms tend to be small, the material and labour costs will run between $3,000 and $5,000. Bathroom repairs and fixes are expensive, but a beautiful one allows you to compete with homes in your area and gets you a higher AVR.

Too Few Bedrooms: When you have bigger bedrooms, try dividing them to add new ones. Additional rooms after repair can increase the value of your investment and help it compete with high-priced properties near you.

Whenever someone buys a property, fixes it, improves its overall value, and then refinance, they are borrowing against the value of that property at the highest rate possible. When executed correctly, this method will allow them to recover most, if not all, of their money invested in the property.

People make something whenever they buy things using their own money. Most lenders nowadays finance seventy-five percent of a property's value, so holders should naturally aim for that. However, experts recommend that holders should stick with the seventy percent instead of seventy-five due to two primary reasons: first, refinancing costs money, and second, aiming for seventy-five percent value of the property offers no contingency to its holders. Options such as cash, hard money loans, private loans, or seller financing can help when purchasing BRRRR property. Choosing between those solely depends on the investor, but they need to carefully account for acquisition and holding costs to ensure that it will hit your seventy or seventy-five percent goal.

The key to success in the BRRRR method is to make sure that you never invest more than seventy-five percent of the property after repair value (ARV). This will make sure that you will never run out of money and can continue purchasing properties.

REHAB

There are two things to consider when rehabbing a rental property. First, you need to make it functional and habitable and, second, you need to make it in a way that the property will increase its value. Correctly rehabbing ensures that your investment will return along with some profit. So unless you are renting out a luxury property, things such as hot tubs, chandeliers, granite countertops, hardwood floors, bay windows, and skylights are not needed. The property also needs to be in good shape, with its primary features in working condition.

Most investors choose properties that need massive repairs since most buyers ignore it, forcing its sellers to drop their prices.

RENT

Most banks do not refinance unoccupied properties, so renting them out should come first. It is necessary to screen your tenants diligently to ensure that they will pay each month. It is also important for the tenants to have a presentable appearance at least; bank appraisers are still human, and they won't refinance a property if its tenants look like they have a questionable background. So before the appraiser comes, make sure to notify your tenants about the visit so they can prepare themselves in advance. Tenants aren't usually required to be present during the visit but, they should clean up and kennel their pets while they are not at home.

The first thing to remember about the BRRRR strategy is that the mortgage will be slightly higher than the traditional method since you are borrowing more money against the property. However, the risks are worth it since bank capital can be used to increase your wealth while the use for the property's equity is limited. The only problem here is that your cash flow will become slightly lower because of the high mortgage payment.

REFINANCE

Before, it was hard to find a bank that is more than willing to refinance single-family rental properties, unlike now.

However, there are things to consider before choosing the bank. First, they should have a cash-out option and, second, they should have a seasoning period, and banks that are willing to lend on the appraised value as soon as the property has been occupied is the best choice.

In looking for great BRRRR banks, it is better to ask those who truly know. Banks that lend to another investor will most likely lend you their money also. The trick to becoming successful here is to make sure that you get the highest appraisal value possible.

REPEAT

Being the most fun part of the BRRRR method, take everything you learned, practiced, changed, and improved, then do it again to another rental property right from step one. You can also work on building systems, which will help you accomplish your objectives by repeating the entire process. The more documented and detailed your systems are, the less you will ever worry about the details most investors miss, overlook, and forget about.

DEVELOPING EXIT STRATEGIES FOR YOUR RENTAL PROPERTIES WHEN SOMETHING GOES WRONG

People invest in real estate because of its financial benefits. Thus the point of purchasing a property is making money through appreciation or consistent cash flow. With this in mind, an investor needs to establish an efficient business plan that includes an exit strategy before purchasing a real estate property.

As the name suggests, an investor's real estate exit strategy is an emergency move to immediately get him out from a possible investment loss.

Some investors usually develop their exit strategy as part of their original investment plan, but others consider creating it once they get a clearer view of the investment. Nevertheless, it is still best to prepare before deciding to take a dip into the investment waters.

THE IMPORTANCE OF AN EXIT STRATEGY IN REAL ESTATE INVESTING

Here are some of the reasons that trigger a real estate investor to implement an exit strategy plan.

An appropriate real estate exit strategy will provide the investor with an action plan and minimize the risks of losses. When a property investor starts developing an ext. strategy before starting investment, then it means that they had explored all possibilities, including the risk associated with the investment and therefore is ready to deal with it.

Implementing an appropriate exit strategy is crucial to success as it will maximize profits. Therefore, it is wise to enter a real estate investing deal once you understand how you will profit once you get out of the agreement. It can save you money throughout your real estate investing career.

Having a prepared exit strategy can prove helpful when you realized that real estate investing is not suitable for you and you had lost your passion. If you cannot keep with real estate investing demands and find it a burden and not worth all your efforts, you can quickly get out without losing your investment with a specific exit plan on hand.

There are situations when you will desperately need cash once a catastrophe strikes. With an exit strategy already installed, it can help you sell the property for liquidation.

For investors who are considering scaling their investment portfolio, having an exit strategy can be beneficial.

Therefore, failing to establish a real estate exit strategy can reduce your potential profits while increasing risks.

HOW TO CHOOSE THE BEST EXIT STRATEGY

Choosing the best real estate investing exit strategies to use is not easy as it seems, and there is no rule to differentiate which one is the best.

In planning an exit strategy, there are many factors to consider, mainly their familiarity with e following:

- Experience

- Investing goals (short and long-term)

- Market condition

- Purchase price

- Market value

- Supply and demand

- Financing options

- Profit potential

- Property condition

Having a clear understanding of these factors and their effects on your investment will allow the real estate investor to determine which exit strategy to adopt.

Factors that may Ruin an Exit Strategy

It is crucial for real estate investors to know that certain factors can harm your exit strategy like,

- Tenants issues

- Depreciation

- Unexpected maintenance cost which may cancel out profits

- Poor property management can reduce the value of an investment and potential cash flow

Nonetheless, an excellent real estate investor can avoid potential obstacles and counteract these potential obstacles by having multiple exit strategies. Anything can change anytime that having a backup plan is a good idea. With various exit strategies, real estate investors can counteract these potential obstacles. Things can change at any given moment; thus, having a backup plan is indeed a good idea.

Therefore, before making a real estate investing deal and acquiring real property, you should have a plan that will allow you to get out of the investment to avoid loss and gain profit, which is the ultimate investment goal.

CHAPTER 4: ANALYZING YOUR INVESTMENT

An investor needs to ascertain the most realistic income that the target property can generate on a sustainable basis throughout the year. What matters most are the historical income figures. When you have an income range, it can serve as your basis in calculating the target property gross rental yield and price-earnings valuation and make a comparison with competitors in the area.

When interest rates go down, rental properties are becoming more valuable. Therefore it requires much bigger capital.

If you want to invest in rental property, you have to make sure that it is the right one to invest in. But how can you guarantee that that the property you want to invest in will generate a profit or even just a sufficient income to cover all its expenses?

This is where you will need rental property analysis. Rental property analysis is the method of analyzing the investment property to determine if it is viable for renting out and determining if it can be a good source of income.

To analyze the viability of the property, you have to consider many factors and metrics. Some of these factors may directly affect the performance of the income property, while others can be used as metrics to gauge its performance and calculate returns on investment.

THE PROPERTY'S POTENTIAL TO GENERATE PROFIT

LOCATION

The location of the income property can directly impact its performance and will dictate your marketing strategy, along with the types of tenants you want to have or want to attract. For example, you target a property near the center of the metropolis. It means that you want to target customers who can afford to rent high-valued homes or commercial spaces.

So even at the start, you will have to set up the goal that you will primarily consider when choosing your location.

Before finally choosing the property, be sure to check on the area and take time to gather the information that you can't easily find on the internet. Also, try to know about how the property and rents have changed over the years.

Rental Strategy

Make sure that you have a specific goal. Will you rent out the property to short-term or long-term tenants? Study the competition in the area. What are the offers to gauge the kind of competition you will get into once you start investing?

Target Tenants

Based on your rental strategy and location, decide on the type of tenants you will offer your property to. There are many strategies you can use to entice tenants. However, you must choose the best one that will work on the type of tenants you are targeting.

PERFORM A COMPARATIVE MARKET ANALYSIS (CMA)

After gathering information, you have to perform a comparative analysis on the property – looking into other properties within the area to determine the fair market value of the property. A fair market value is a determined value of an asset or property based on its likely sales price to a third-party buyer. Simply put, it is the reasonable amount the buyer would pay to purchase the property or any asset at a given period. In real estate, determining the fair market value does not only depend on the comparable market analysis of price based on the broker's opinion, but it likewise takes into account what the free market is willing to pay for it.

One way is to look into the most recent comparable property deal to be able to come up with a potential acquisition price you may offer. Doing a Comparable Market Analysis will give you a fair estimate of the property value when analyzing metrics. As the name suggests, a comparative market analysis is looking through similar properties in the area. This way, you can determine the fair market value of the property. You may also look into recently sold comparable properties, referred to as **comps,** to come up with a potential price that you can use in your offer. Moreover, doing a market price analysis will provide you with a fair estimate of the value of the property when analyzing financial metrics such as the **cap rate**.

FINDING THE RIGHT INVESTMENT PROPERTY DATA

Finally, let us take a look at the right information on your investment property. In commercial real estate, the seller would provide potential buyers with a **pro forma,** an informative resource material that provides information about the property, like the amount of rental income that the property generates every month. While it is not a common practice in residential properties, it won't hurt to ask the seller for details.

Remember that any information, especially figures provided to you by the seller, is shown in their best light, so it is best that you do your own due diligence. You may find rental income data in public property records in your local **Multiple Listing Service (MLS)**.

ANALYZING METRICS

Having all the needed data, you can look at the metrics that will be useful for you in making informed choices. Such data will help you determine if the property is a profitable investment. One important metric to use is the **Net Operating Income (NOI).**

When analyzing metrics, your first step should be finding the NOI for the property. Net Operating Income or NOI is a measure of income that the property will generate after operating expenses are deducted. While NOI will not give you a full view of the property's profitability, it forms the basis for many other equations that you will use in your investment analysis.

Here's the formula for Net Operating Income.

NOI = Rental Income + Other Income – Operating Expenses

While a large part of your income will come from the monthly rental, don't include income from other sources like income from laundry facilities and parking fees. Expenses like utilities, maintenance, and other regular expenses should be part of operating expenses. With regard to the mortgage payment, it is not part of these expenses, and Net Operation Income does not take into account debt service.

After determining your Net Operating Income, it's time that you calculate your Cash on Cash Return which we discussed in another chapter. Your Cash on Cash Return or Return on Investment (ROI) will tell you your return relative to the amount of money you will be investing acquiring the property. Take note to include the cost of any repairs, closing costs, other startup expenses in calculating your initial investment.

Each investor has their own way of doing a market analysis. Nonetheless, this information will give you a good starting point for your market analysis. While equipped with all the necessary information you need, you are now to make an informed choice as to whether the property that you are interested in will be a profitable real estate property investment.

CHAPTER 5: DAY-TO-DAY OPERATIONS

L andlords carry many duties and responsibilities. Their tasks involve more than just looking for tenants or collecting rent. They are also custodians, troubleshooters, conflict solvers, negotiators, supervisors, counsellors, and business people. Landlords should have the knowledge of how to:

- Attract property inspectors and tenants

- Handle the rental property and tenants

- Deal with angry tenants and neighbours

Being a landlord needs to know, understand, and follow the law— whether state-wide or national landlord-tenant regulations. These rules include following safety and health standards, collecting security deposits, evicting tenants, and being a live-in landlord.

Below are several points you need to know as a landlord:

PROPERTY MANAGEMENT

Safety is of supreme importance before a landlord installs tenants in a rental property since they are responsible for keeping them safe. Failure to do so can lead you to penalties or land you in prison.

You are required to make sure that the property's amenities are up-to-standard, secured, and safe. To determine whether your property is fit for the tenants, here are the areas you need to check:

- Drainage and sanitary facilities

- Freedom from the damp

- Food preparation and cooking facilities

- Water supply

- Wastewater disposal

- Ventilation and natural lighting

- Repair and stability

- Safety and security amenities

Rental properties with grave issues such as damp, inadequate heating, mould, and pest infestations fall short of the government's standards. As a landlord, you must take proper measures to meet all the requirements before accepting any tenants. Should the tenants point out any issues in the unit you rent out, you must take steps to fix those problems.

Ensuring that the property you rent out is safe is not a complex matter. For the most part, you only need to implement common sense. Consider the rental property as your own home, and put yourself in your tenants' shoes. What areas should you improve to make it habitable and comfortable for the tenants? Do the walls have any signs of moulds? Can you hear mice scuttling here and there? If you were a tenant, would you live in it?

Fix any issues that could be considered a safety problem. See to it that there are fire safety devices such as fire alarms and CO (carbon monoxide) detectors. Let experts check the electrical installations and plumbing to ensure that there would be no concealed hazards that may cause significant problems. If there are gas appliances present, provide your tenants with a Gas Safety certificate.

If you would not want to spend even a night in your rental property, then it is more likely that nobody else would be happy to live there. Furthermore, well-maintained properties can command higher rent and high-quality tenants.

When you already addressed the safety and maintenance issues, it is wise to spruce up the unit before marketing it. You can give the walls a new paint to liven up the place. Many landlords prefer neutral tones instead of vivid ones since these attract the majority of the prospective tenants.

FINDING SUITABLE TENANTS

Marketing the property is a crucial part of the self-management process. There are many methods that you could use in finding tenants for your rental business property. But before employing any method, you should consider the location and category of your rental property first. There may be no specific method that you could use for all locations. However, there are considered suitable locations for certain regions.

Many people tend to look out for a tenant finder package instead of a letting agent. Nowadays, the digital platform is a friend to any landlord who aims to keep in touch with prospective clients directly.

FINDING TENANTS FOR YOUR PROPERTY YOURSELF

If your rental property lies in New York City, for most people, the assistance of a broker is the most common way of getting your property rented. But if not, other than or instead of contacting a real estate agent to get your property listed on the MLS, you could personally enlist your rental property.

You could enlist your property in any of the following platforms:

Zillow Rental Manager

You will be charged $9.99 for using this platform. As a perk, it will also list your post on HotPads and Trulia.

Cozy.co

Cozy.co is a free-listing platform that works side-by-side with Doorsteps.com and Realtor.com

Craiglist

Social Media Networks

You can take advantage of the power of social media when looking for tenants. Join communities created specifically for linking people who are interested in rental properties. You may also advertise on Instagram, Facebook, Twitter, etc.

With these sites, you'll most probably have lots of viewers for your rental property even without the help of agents.

You do not want people to discourage people right away with exorbitant prices. Make sure to make your rent competitive in the current market. Charge according to the value you offer. Additionally, targeting the right demographic gives you an edge in the competition.

The first step in marketing your property is to prepare your materials. Since you are going digital, good photos will be your ace card. If you lack photography skills, hire a professional to take the photos— it is quite a brilliant investment. Generally, letting agents make use of the freelance photographers' skills so, there is no reason you cannot use this tactic.

To ensure that the photos look good inside and out, schedule your photoshoot during a sunny day. Pictures are also best taken shortly after renovating and decorating a property. As long as you do not make any significant changes, you can reuse these photos each time you need to market the property. For this reason, professional shots are always a sound investment.

If your budget is limited, you can utilize various ways to market your property. For one, stick to the leading property portals such as:

- Airbnb

- Realtor Canada

- Re/Max

- Zolo

- Point2Homes

However, some websites do not allow landlords to add their listings directly. They need to register with an online letting agent. In this case, you can try sites such as Owner Direct and RENTCafé. There are also sites like Kijiji, Craigslist, and RentSeeker.

Besides these online platforms, you can also try print marketing campaigns for the older generation who might not use social media. Try placing business cards in community centers or bulletin boards in shops. Another strategy is to put a sign outside the property with your contact information. This way, anyone walking past your property can get in touch with you. You can also place an ad in local newspapers if you want to.

Another marketing method, which usually brings about great results, is word of mouth. Tell everyone you know about the property you are renting up, and ask them to spread the word. If you have existing tenants, persuade them to tell their friends, family, and acquaintances that you have a property or unit for rent. You can sweeten the deal by offering them a referral fee.

TENANT REFERENCING

Tenant referencing refers to a landlord's or letting agent's way of seeking information about a prospective tenant to weigh their decisions, whether to accept the prospect or not. The process is quite challenging and critical. You cannot simply assume that they can be high-quality tenants because they behave politely and drive a good-looking car. A flashy individual sometimes only has $50 in their bank account. A seemingly nice person with a brilliant smile can sometimes be a sex offender. Tenant referencing can lessen these risks you have to face being a landlord.

Understand that appearances can be quite deceptive, and the only way to ascertain that your prospective tenant is the same as he or she declares is to conduct tenant referencing. You need to check a prospect's basic personal information, such as their:

- Personal information

- Contact details

- Previous landlord details

- Financial history

- Employment details

- Income information

- Guarantees

Ask a prospective tenant to fill up a questionnaire before anything else. Call the prospect's employer or former landlord to check whether what they claim is reliable or otherwise. Check them on social media; you will be surprised how much information you can acquire with their digital behaviour.

If you want to dig deeper, you can avail yourself of tenant screening services. They can perform criminal background checks, eviction history, credit reports, and verify a previous landlord's references. If you want peace of mind, paying professional tenant screening services is an excellent investment.

However, it is crucial to understand that you cannot select or refuse tenants based on the following:

- Place of origin or ethnic origin

- Race and colour

- Sex or sexual orientation

- Religion

- Age

- Marital or family status

- Disability or handicap

As a landlord, you should never ask prospective tenants questions that could be interpreted as such during the selection process. Questions pertaining to the prospect's sexual preference, faith, or plans to have more children are considered taboo.

LEASE CONTRACTS

A lease contract is a legal, written rental agreement that summarizes everything a landlord and a tenant have agreed to. Standard rental agreements are designed for the interests of both the landlord and tenant. Generally, it contains the following areas:

Duration of Agreement

Rental periods typically last for 12 months, at which time the landlord cannot increase the rent. It is crucial to keep in mind the notice periods that either landlord or the tenant has to provide in order to terminate the contract.

Responsibility for Utility Costs

Be clear about which household services will be included in the rent and those which the tenants have to pay for themselves. It is best for both you and the tenants to be as detailed as possible.

Deposit

The majority of rental contracts in Canada entail the tenant to pay the first and last month's rent in advance. The reason for this is for the landlord to collect the deposit that will be used for any damages you created, together with any debts the tenants have incurred by the end of their tenancy. It is often advisable that the landlord and the tenant inspect the property and write down an inventory on the first day of the tenancy.

Forfeiture

The landlord has the right to evict the tenant if they committed a breach of contract.

LANDLORD INSURANCE

Owning a rental property is a significant investment, and as a landlord, there are certain risks you have to face. If you own an apartment, rental house, or rental condominium, it is only wise to consider availing enough insurance.

Rental insurance will help you secure and protect your property from numerous issues. It can cover any damages to your property from unforeseen events such as fire and water damages. Liability insurance, for one, can help in case someone is injured on your rental property. If you want to protect your property and your tenants, rental insurance is a must.

THE DIFFERENCE BETWEEN RENTAL INSURANCE AND HOME INSURANCE

Rental insurance and home insurance are two different policies. Your home insurance policy cannot cover your rental properties. Likewise, your rental insurance policy coverage does not include your own home.

Home insurance covers personal liability and property and the contents in your residence. It also includes the structure of your house and your belongings. Most home insurance policies cover a standard range of typical perils for your dwelling. Here are some of the most common hazards covered by the policy:

- Windstorm

- Hail

- Fire

- Smoke

- Water damage

- Snow, ice, and sleet

- Vehicle

- Lightning

- Explosion

- Burglary

- Vandalism

- Riot or civil unrest

- Trees and other falling objects

When you move out and rent out space to a tenant, you need to switch to rental insurance. Rental insurance varies from other types of home insurance policies. So, if you are contemplating becoming a landlord, you have to acquire specific insurance for your rental property to protect it from damage. The insurance covers the physical aspect of the property you are renting out as well as its liability coverage.

LIMITING PERSONAL LIABILITY WITH LEGAL ENTITIES

Many residential landlords are considered to be high-profile targets in legal circles. The leading reason for this is their ignorance and utter disregard for the standards mandated by the government. They run their business with little to no regard for their tenants' safety and best interests. For them, their obligation involves giving the tenants a living space and collect rent.

These landlords act like loan sharks dressed in flashy dresses or suits and equally striking foreign automobiles. They are also the same who are awfully underinsured and entirely clueless about diminishing their risks and limiting their personal liabilities as landlords. If you do not want to be cannon fodder in court, the best approach to running your residential business is to keep it modest.

A low-key approach entails honest, reliable, ethical, and professional dealing. This manner keeps you and your business away from single-minded code enforcement officials, prying members of the media, green-eyed tenants, and sue-happy plaintiff's lawyers eager for some quick cash. The rental business is always in cutthroat competition, after all.

There are three basic types of insurance coverage every landlord should carry:

Property Coverage

It protects you financially against any damages caused to the property's structures and any landlord-owned items.

Liability Coverage

This policy covers any injury or damage to someone on the property. For example, you are liable to cover for a tenant who slipped and falls because of the water leak you should be responsible for maintaining. The coverage may also protect you in the event that the tenant sues you for damages.

Rental Default Insurance

Issues such as severe termite and pest infestation, mould, and a sinkhole can render your property uninhabitable. Any tenant cannot enjoy living in a unit with these problems. On your part, it is illegal to rent out your property, knowing that your property has any of these conditions. Rental default insurance offers coverage on the rental fees you should have collected only if these issues are not present, making your property unfit for occupancy.

OTHER OPTIONAL LANDLORD INSURANCE COVERAGE

You may want to enhance your coverage beyond the basics of your landlord insurance. Depending on what is included in the package, you may want to add extra features such as:

APPLIANCES

Large appliances come with a hefty price tag, and therefore, are considered another enormous investment. Replacing them can drain your pocket. Appliance insurance policy can cover any major appliances like washing machines, dryers, refrigerators, stoves, air conditioning, etc.

WATER DAMAGE PROTECTION

Water damage is one of the top threats to property owners. It is often caused by burst pipes, storm waters, accumulated rainwater, leaking appliances, spring thaw, and other freshwater flooding types.

VANDALISM

If your rental property is vandalized, this kind of damage is not typically covered by the standard landlord insurance.

BURGLARY OR THEFT

The traditional landlord insurance policy may help you repair your home when any break-in damages happen. However, it will not replace any stolen items. The burglary coverage will help you in this issue. With this policy, you can easily replace your stolen items.

BUILDING CODES

The county or city code authorities may require you to upgrade items, such as electrical wiring and ventilation, when you repair or replace any damaged part of your rental property. The reason behind this requirement is that the codes may have changed since your property was originally built. This type of insurance coverage helps you refund those additional costs.

RENTAL PROPERTY UNDER CONSTRUCTION

If you are renovating or gutting your property for improvement, you may have to purchase supplementary coverage to protect its structure until it is ready to be inhabited.

ADDING VALUE TO YOUR PROPERTY

According to Harvard's Joint Center for Housing Studies, estimates on Americans' total spending on remodelling houses is expected to rise from $332 billion in the 2nd quarter of 2020 to $337 billion until the 2nd quarter of 2021.

As the pandemic drags on, 76 percent of real estate agents claim that home renovations are on the rise. When the economy is not secure, people would rather rent than buy a house. Because of the increasing demand for rental properties, the competition in home rentals is likewise going up. As a rental property investor, you wouldn't want to be stuck with a property with no tenant. The key then is to make your property competitive, and the way to do it is to upgrade it.

Here are some remodelling project recommendations aimed to increase the value of your home.

CREATE A FEELING OF ADDING MORE SPACE

Regardless of their income, people want a home with ample space. This desire for a home with bigger space gained momentum in the wake of the 2020 global pandemic. Create more Space

Another mark of a modern home is lighter, brighter, and more communal spaces. It would do a lot to open floor plans, especially on the first floor. You may transform a door to become an archway or remove a wall that's not load-bearing and make sure you leave a support column. Most importantly, ask a structural engineer's opinion before demolishing a portion of those concrete structures.

When thinking of increasing your home value, it's not always making a major renovation on your kitchen or flooring. Deteriorating windows, especially when they are leaking, can be a deal-breaker for potential tenants. New windows will not only improve the appearance of your property but may likewise save on your utility bills.

Everyone prefers a greener home that's low on utility bills which only means that energy efficiency impacts the prices of a property.

BOOST YOUR CURB APPEAL

In real estate, pricing has little to do with how much you paid for the property or how much you spent improving it. Values and rents are based on how the tenant perceives the value of the property.

Appearance matters for potential tenants that a minor alteration could create a drastic impact on the functionality of the property or build an image of luxury. In short, to make your property more competitive, manage the tenant's first impression by making your property a convenient place to live. One way to kick up your curb appeal is to create a well-groomed loan or house paint that's neither faded nor flaky, at the minimum.

You don't need to stop there. A good landscape or a beautiful garden can create a great first impression. Consider planting a hedge or purchase potted bushes and line them up where you want them to create a little privacy.

If you don't want to break the bank, simply line the pathway or home entrance with potted plants.

There's no quicker way to increase the value of your property once you boost its curb appeal.

REPAIR OR REPLACE THE ROOF

While we are talking about curb appeal, another way of increasing your property value is replacing or fixing the roof. Even when you paint your home, if there are water damages due to leaks from the roof, it won't do anything better to improve your home appeal.

The roof is one of the many things that will determine the value of your home. Once your roof needs some fixing, it will immediately go to the "fixer-upper category."

You must take into consideration the age of the roof when deciding whether to replace or repair roofing. It could be more cost-effective in the long run to replace a leaking roof rather than just fix it.

Style matters when changing windows, but it can also be expensive. So, try to research some designs that will be worth your money and not just empty your pocket or break your bank.

If you're a handyman, you may save money on installation costs by doing it yourself or if you are hiring someone, make sure that you negotiate for the lowest price possible. Replacing your windows will not only raise the value of your home but will also appreciate its marketability once you decide to list it on the market.

ADD MORE BATHROOM

A property with many bathrooms reassured tenants or renters that they don't have to get in line when they need to use it. It is also a park of modernization as opposed to the traditional one bathroom per house. Today, people build their homes with several bathrooms. But because adding a bathroom can get expensive, rerouting pipes, ensure you know where the plumbing runs through the house and if it is possible to add more bathrooms where you want them to.

CREATE ANOTHER BEDROOM

Many would agree that a bedroom can't classify as a bedroom without a closet. However, legally, it doesn't speak so (Ericson, 2020).

But adding a closet could add more definition to your bedroom. It could simply mean adding small drywall, but when listing your home as a three-bedroom house makes a big difference compared to listing a two-bedroom house for a new bedroom can easily add a hundred dollars to your rental price.

So, when spotting for properties, keep an eye on these bonus rooms. It will be great to buy a two-bedroom house and then convert it into a three-bedroom home a few days after.

So if you bought a house with an exceptionally large master's bedroom, you might split it up to make it two by building drywall in between.

The number of bedrooms is a primary driver of the value of the real property. Therefore, adding one is the fastest way to increase your property value and add equity to your property.

RENOVATIONS

Renovating your rental property to increase rental income doesn't mean you need to break the bank, as there are plenty of ways to ensure you're keeping up with the competitive market.

To save money and worries, one trick you need to learn is to have a different approach to renovating your rental property from how you would approach it when you're remodelling your own home. Although you may have your preferences, the rental market would not require you to apply the same intricate attention to detail. I'm not saying that you should completely overlook the details. However, you should pay more attention to those minor fixes that have the most significant impact on your rental business.

Consider the following instead of improving the appearance.

REPLACE ANYTHING BROKEN

A landlord's priority must be on fixing anything that's broken in your rental property, like a malfunctioning doorknob, locks, or a leaking faucet. Also include changing the current showerhead is subpar to the water pressure. These fixes are no expensive but can make your rental investment alluring to prospective tenants.

UPDATE FLOORING

Some things need no replacement, like when you have carpet on your flooring. All you need is a professional carpet cleaning service, and you can give your old carpet-covered flooring a whole new light. However, keep in mind that with hardwood flooring, tenants typically see hardwood flooring as a desirable quality when looking for a place to rent and much easier to clean than a carpet. Furthermore, suitable flooring that is easy to clean could be a deciding factor for potential tenants, especially when they have kids or pets.

Vinyl and tile flooring could also be good options for flooring. Other affordable choices are ceramic and laminate flooring.

PAINT THE WALLS

Most landlords consider it the best practice to paint the interior walls of your rental property, which offers plenty of aesthetic appeal for potential tenants when marketing your property. Repainting walls also allow you to keep track of any wear and tear. Use neutral colours in your painting enough to complete varying decoration designs.

CONSIDER MONITOR LANDSCAPING

If you have a rental property with ground-level entry, a porch, or a yard, doing some minor landscaping can be an added finishing touch that can provide a relaxed ambiance to your property. Remember that an aesthetically pleasing exterior entices any walk-in tenants in the same way that an unkempt or untidy exterior can deter potential renters.

RENTAL PROPERTY MAINTENANCE

Owning a rental property involves routine maintenance to maintain continuous cash flow every year. Landlords must keep their tenants happy and their properties in optimal condition by investing a part of their income into routine maintenance.

In countries experiencing four seasons, routine maintenance might mean a lot of work, but they are vital to ensure that your property does not decay or break down rapidly. Starting with spring, one must make sure to minimize moisture damage as much as possible. In summer, one must prepare the outdoor areas for warm-weather activities while initiating pest control inside the house at the same time.

Animal control is the primary concern during fall since animals instinctively seek warm shelter, making your property an ideal place. And lastly, winterizing your property during winter is a must to prevent the cold from getting in. Accomplishing these things requires a constant reminder to keep one's rental property in great shape as much as possible.

Keep in mind, however, that the tenants also have their share of responsibility in maintaining the property in shape. After all, they are the ones who directly benefit from the well-maintained property. Their help will lessen your burden and make the property more suitable for them to live in.

SPRING MAINTENANCE TASKS

Landscape Management

Doing this will increase your property's overall appearance as well as keeping your place accident-free due to possible debris brought by winter storms. Pruning tree branches and shrubs also keep your roofing and siding moisture-free, as well as preventing insects and vermin from finding their way inside your house. Moving the lawn and planting flowers are also good springtime ideas since they enhance your property's beauty.

Minimizing Moisture

Mould buildup inside and outside the house means excess moisture, which will also cause your property to decay faster if left unchecked.

You can prevent mildew buildup inside the house by installing a dehumidifier or hiring people who offer such a service.

If mould buildup has penetrated the unit's structure, make sure to hire a professional to address the problem.

Inspecting the Heating System

A heating system performs during winter as much as possible to keep the whole house heated, which could also lead to potential issues when ignored. However, checking the heating system out is best done during springtime since it is also the time wherein a heating system is used minimally. Make sure that the heating pipes are clean and free of leaks as much as possible.

Gutter Cleaning

This is an important task before and after wet seasons since winter can bring debris that becomes trapped in gutters, eventually resulting in leaks. Whenever a leak occurs, it could cause extensive damage to the interior, causing the landlord much stress along with expenses.

SUMMER MAINTENANCE TASKS

Pest Control

For breeding purposes, bugs and other insects like ants, spiders, flies, mosquitoes, and wasps like warm weather for breeding purposes. Treating your property with pesticides or hiring pest control professionals is a good move since leaving those bugs alone will cause problems like disease and inconvenience. Wasps also have stings that can probably cause paralysis, allergic reactions, or even death, depending on the amount of poison injected inside the victim's body.

Fire Prevention Preparedness

High temperatures could easily start a fire, which is one of the reasons why summer is also known as the fire prevention season in most countries. Landlords and tenants alike should keep their property less of a fire hazard by trimming bushes or trees, which could become a fire vector. Make sure to check the property for potential gas leaks and household chemicals that could cause fire, such as chlorine or fuels like kerosene and gasoline.

Checking in with Tenants

Landlords can use this time to properly communicate with tenants and address various issues such as rent adjustment, maintenance, contract renewals, etc. You can do this by organizing a simple party or dinner and asking them about such matters when opportunity calls it. You can also offer more incentives such as free Wi-Fi connection, lower rent, and much more to encourage them to stay longer.

Checking Sprinkler Systems

Water supply should be conserved during summer as much as possible, so make sure to program sprinkler systems to operate as per existing water rationing regulations. Check the pipes for potential leaks and damage to reduce standing water on your landscape.

Readying Outdoor Needs/Amenities

Summertime is also a season of having fun. Amenities like grills, fire pits, pools, and tents should be kept clean and ready for use as much as possible. Keep your tenants happy by providing some space for enjoyment and leisure.

AUTUMN MAINTENANCE TASKS

Fall Safety Inspection

Autumn is associated with both rain and cold weather, so make sure that the handrails in your property are well-placed and can keep anyone from slipping or falling on wet surfaces.

Animal Control and Proofing

Cold weather can also potentially bring animals inside your home looking for warm shelter so make sure to reinforce or seal potential animal entrances inside your home using wire or steel meshes when doing some animal proofing. If raccoons, squirrels, or wild animals find their way inside your home, make sure to contact animal control as soon as possible.

Exterior Checks

Check your property for inexpensive maintenance issues like roof and gutter cleaning, caulking, or debris removal. Fixing minor issues before they become more extensive is the key to minimizing maintenance issues.

Attic Preparation

Make sure that your property's attic insulation is in good condition to prevent ice from building up on your roof. Doing this prevents the roof from sustaining considerable damage during winter, which will also prevent expensive repairs from coming.

Caulking

Caulking or sealing is an important task done during summertime. It can also be done by the landlord or tenants alone, which makes it inexpensive. Sealing leaks or openings prevents water from getting in and freezing, which can damage the entire structure.

Roof Inspection

Roofs get easily damaged when exposed to rapidly changing temperatures and weather. Even a lost shingle or roof tile could cause deterioration to your property's insulation, wood, drywall, plumbing, heating, and electrical systems when ignored. Checking these issues out is better done during summer rather than in the middle of winter. Since roofing is very important, make sure to hire a professional to check the condition of your roof on an annual basis.

Gutter Cleaning

Leaves and branches fall in huge quantities during autumn, hence the term 'fall.' Small and fragile as they may seem, dried leaves and branches can clog gutters with ease. To prevent this from happening as well as water from flowing inside your property, regularly cleaning it is a must.

WINTER MAINTENANCE TASKS

Prune Trees and Clear Debris

Protect your vegetation from harsh weather by pruning it. Doing this will also protect your tenants from debris that could probably fall because of winter storms since ice and snow buildup can break the most fragile branches. Such things can become an obstacle, and mulching leaves make roads slippery.

Winterize Pipes

Water and Heating pipes should be insulated to keep them from bursting or freezing when the temperature suddenly drops. Disconnect garden hoses, insulate outdoor spigots and keep a faucet or two running slowly to prevent the water line from freezing. Also, keep the kitchen cabinet door open, allowing warm air to flow around the pipes.

Flush/Drain the Water Heater

According to experts, you should flush or drain the heater pipes at least every two years to prevent mineral buildup that will potentially affect its efficiency. Old water heaters require more attention: if some of their parts are already damaged, make sure to have them repaired or replaced.

Check the Roof

Hire a roofing professional when it comes to checking your rental property's roof for possible problems. It is necessary to check even the slightest damage since it can become bigger once the winter storm strikes. And once the roof damages become bigger, it could leave your plumbing, insulation, interior, and heating systems vulnerable to weathering.

Weather-Proof Structures

Insulate and seal windows against winter chill to keep your rental property's heating costs as low as possible. Insulations prevent heat from escaping through leaks and cracks, making heating the entire home interior easier.

ADDITIONS

CHAPTER 6: DEALING WITH TENANTS

HOW TO DEAL WITH PROBLEM TENANTS

As you begin your journey in managing rental properties, you will inevitably encounter problem tenants and deal with them. Most of the time, property managers and owners rely on intensive tenant screening as their solution to sift out the good from the bad applicants and to be able to protect their business. But still, bad tenants could find loopholes on screenings and get through until they get to lease your property.

For instance, a tenant may have shown to be a reliable rent payer before but has been beginning to miss their dues because they face financial difficulties. Another might be a troubled tenant who may have passed screening but then paints your walls neon pink and gets a huge pig as their pet, or worse, someone who is a chronic complainer, who pushes your wit's end because of unceasing demands. No screening systems invented could detect such notorious tenants.

Here are common types of problem renters and pieces of advice on how to deal with them.

Late or Partial-Paying Renters

Of all issues related to tenants, the most common is paying late or partial.

Be a wise manager. Make it very clear with your tenants in a friendly way that your system for property management is rigid -that you don't tolerate late payments, or the accountant will be accountable for delinquent dues in the cash flow at the end of the year. You could also say that they would have to shoulder the penalty that goes with the accounting system (though you would have to ready yourself for numerous pleading and begging phone calls). On top of these things, your tenants should never get the idea that penalties for late payments are negotiable. They can't take advantage of your generosity if you don't give them a chance to do it.

Even if you made everything clear and made means to protect your business, expect that a time would come, you'll have to face it – partial, late, or no payment at all. So, the best advice that you could get is to be firm whatever personality you might have, or they have. If not, it's an open invitation for getting into future trouble. Today, it's maybe only three days late, but next time, it will be three weeks late. So don't risk it. If you haven't advised them about late dues being irrevocable, now is the time to say it.

If the rent payment – whether late or partial – came to the point where the lease states to perform the necessary action, call or email the tenant a few days before time. It will serve as a polite warning for them. This warning, which will likewise serve as a notice for those who don't pay their rent, comes with a specific timetable. They have to leave if they refuse to pay. When that day comes, do the necessary action even when you feel uncomfortable doing it.

If you're the manager, it will be easier for you to become strict with the tenants since you're not the owner. You could tell them that the owner sets the rules and not you. But still, being soft with your tenants is not advisable even if you're the owner. Just think about those unfortunate renters who turn to their friends, family, or another source and not their landlords. They have other options. Let them turn to them.

Wrecking Balls

Property damage is the second most common problem with tenants.

In this case, a mobile inspection app is convenient and beneficial instead of the standard clipboard. Not only could it cut your inspection time by more than 50%, but it also enables you to take photos and place that in your inspection report. If ever your property acquires damage, you can show the previous photos as your evidence.

Another issue under property damage is an unapproved improvement made by the tenant that looks more like a distraction for you. Anyway, it depends on you if you'll consider it an improvement or not, but at least, you should indicate in your lease that when they move out of the property, they must leave the property in the condition as it was before they moved in.

Let's say they painted the walls black. They need to repaint it to the original colour before they leave, or they need to pay for its paint restoration that will fall under the damage deposit.

If there is damage, request in writing that the tenant acknowledge the damage and keep a copy in your possession. If the tenant refused or can't handle the damage, let your maintenance people fix it and send the bill to your tenant. Also, indicate in your lease that you have the right to do those actions if your property is beyond use.

It would be advisable to conduct interim inspections during the lease period if you have specific rules like a strict 'no smoking policy. If you think the place would probably have trouble leasing to the next renter, perform the necessary action. If the renter doesn't agree to fixing or paying the maintenance cost, you have the right to kick them out with a 'cure or quit notice. Just be sure you have that already in your lease contract before allowing any move-ins in your property.

Hosts to All

Some renters sublet a part of the whole property itself with or without your permission. It is because nowadays, Airbnb or short-term rental vacations are rising in popularity. Some areas consider short-term rentals illegal, but for some, legal. However, it's not a good idea to let many strangers occupy your rental property, especially when neighbours often tend to ask why they (strangers) are there. Also, they are not the ones whom you screened and approved to be on your property in the first place.

Some houseguests could range from a friend who stays for a weekend (permissible) to a death metal band that lasts for a month-long party celebration (a nuisance probably for the neighbourhood).

So, give your lease more specifications to avoid future problems with unexpected guests. If you don't get specific with your limits for unforeseen guests, your tenants would have a free runway with their guests and tell you that they could do whatever they wish as long as they're paying for it.

Whiners

These renters will constantly call you to make unreasonable requests whenever they like (most likely, they will make one after another). It could range from things that need to be fixed to simple things that they could handle for themselves (as stated in the lease).

What to do with them? Ignore them if the issue is not worth your while. You are not legally obligated to do everything you wish. But it's still up to you if you want to respond to each request they make.

Indulgent Pet Owners Tenants

Animals living at your property can do much damage to it and can also lead to difficulties in finding tenants after a move-out. Thus, it will be much better if you don't make compromises where animals are concerned. For example, a pet dog that chews anything or a cat who wants its territory marked with urine are sure ways to get your property a significant overhaul.

Now, if you allow pets, make sure to inspect your property periodically for acquired damages. If not, but you found evidence of animals in your property, invoke consequences before complications arise or your tenants move out. Take note that under the ADA, service animals are not counted as pets.

Furthermore, there are tenants who have exotic pets, so prepare your answer if you will allow exotic animals or not.

Lawbreakers

Even if you do have the other five problem tenants within your property, you could still consider yourself lucky if you never had a renter who:

- Grows marijuana illegally

- Abuses or sells narcotics

- Gets drunk on the front lawn

- Engages in any illegal activity under your rental property

If you find yourself a tenant, who is a willing lawbreaker, the best way is to evict them or call the police, especially in issues that deal with violence or drug sales. It is the reason why criminal records, aside from financial records, are looked upon in screening services. However, a tenant's arrest doesn't evoke his rights to the property which they legally rented. So ask for an attorney's advice about the eviction you are planning to do.

The problem tenants mentioned are the major ones in the single-family category. You will find specific parking and noise complaints less frequently with single-family properties than with multi-family properties.

When You Want to Finish the Deal

Even if you finally decide to kick problem tenants out of your property, you can't do it, especially if their lease is valid. It would be best if you also didn't resolve to forms of harassment such as turning off the water, changing locks, threatening and driving them out of your property.

But then, eviction will only be applicable for instances like you tried your best to work things out, but nothing changed, or your tenant is involved with illegal activities and the likes. As for those cases, you should go through legalities before you can proceed to evictions.

How to Deal With Problem Tenants

Serve a notice according to your area regulations. Use Certified Mail to ensure that your tenant got it and can't give the 'I never received the letter' for an excuse. Even those renters who show civility can be enraged or desperate when it comes to evictions.

Cooperate with the courts if you have to do evictions. Contact a lawyer specializing in removals and let them guide the proceedings through the regular court system since small courts couldn't handle them.

Get as much evidence as you can. These will be your valid reasons to evict the problem tenant. The court might probably ask you to present them during the proceedings.

If you've been in the rental property business for quite a time, you probably experienced having most (if not all) of these six problem renters. You might even have evicted at least one. Truly, handling such situations is stressful, but you need to protect your territory. Just remember that you're not the only property manager who has been through these scenarios. Many others have been there also, and you could find a lot of good advice from them.

DIFFERENT METHODS FOR COLLECTING RENT

Designing a method for collecting monthly rent makes it easier for you to monitor which of your tenants are behind or up-to-date with their rent. As a landlord, you have to determine which option works best for your current situation.

You can choose from various approaches enumerated below, which suits you well. But before that, let us talk about the factors you must consider when deciding on your rent collection method:

NUMBER OF RENTAL UNITS OR TENANTS

When you own more than ten units, you probably do not prefer to knock on each unit's door to collect the rent. In this case, you will want a more organized and efficient method to collect payments.

DISTANCE FROM YOUR RENTAL PROPERTY

If you live miles away from your rentals, providing the option for electronic transfer or hiring a third-party rent collector will be your best recourse.

PREFERENCE FOR A HANDS-OFF APPROACH

You may only have two or three rental units and live a few minutes away from it, but you would like to maintain less interaction with your tenants. In this case, the mail or electronic funds transfer can be your best choice to obtain your rental.

CONVENIENCE WITH THE USE OF TECHNOLOGY

If you are not comfortable using e-money transfers or any form of wire transfer, you may favour collecting the rent in person.

PAYMENT OPTIONS

You can also base your decisions depending on which payment option you prefer. Keep in mind that not all of these forms are equal. These payment options can be easily verified and are more secure.

Certified Check

Certified checks are bank-issued and serve as proof that the tenant's bank account has the required funds available when the check is written. Nevertheless, it cannot guarantee that those funds are still present in the account by the time you actually deposit the check. Although this form is more secure than a personal check, it is not as secure as a cashier's check.

Cashier's Check

A cashier's check can be compared to a money order but requires a more significant fee. Moreover, they are only issued by the bank where the tenant has an account since it becomes the responsibility of the bank to get the fund from the account of the tenant. They will also guarantee the amount that the cashier's check is for. Because the bank underwrites the amount, you do not have to worry about the funds when you attempt to cash the check.

Money Order

Money orders can be acquired at a convenience store, local post office, or a bank for a small fee. It is a more trusted payment method than a check.

The tenant had to transfer funds to obtain the money order, making it similar to receiving a rent gift card. For instance, the tenant needs a money order of $500. They can go to a post office, bank, or convenience store and exchange the cash for a money order, which they can forward to you.

Online Payment

This payment option does not require you to provide any of your personal banking information to any person, making it a more secure option. It also uses a quick and straightforward method that allows you to receive the funds almost instantly after the tenant has sent the money. Usually, the sender (in this case, the tenant) will only need your email or phone number to send you the money.

Meanwhile, there are also payment options you need to avoid as much as possible. These include:

Cash

Cash is easy to dispute because people often fail to document transactions that involve a small amount of money. A dishonest tenant can claim that they have already paid the rent in cash, but you may realize later on that they are $20 or $50 short. If the total rental amount is not placed in the envelope, you might find yourself in a dispute.

Personal Check

Personal checks are hard to get verified. They may not be accurate, or if the funds are available upon its issue, it does not guarantee that it will not bounce. You can allow your tenant to pay rent with this method upon reaching a certain trust level, which they can obtain after establishing a payment history using a more secure method.

Direct Deposit to Your Bank Account

Do not let your tenants directly deposit their monthly rent into your banking account since this requires you to provide them with your banking details. It can pose a security risk on your part, especially if your tenant is not the "simple" person they claim to be.

Credit Cards

Never allow your tenants to pay you using their credit cards. First, you will be the one shouldering the transaction fee to the credit company. Secondly, the tenant has the opportunity to report the charge as a fraudulent transaction. This situation can be a big headache and a waste of time plus, there is a chance that it may go against your favour.

Based on the abovementioned factors, you can opt for the method that suits your preference. You must insert a clause in the lease agreement that tackles how you collect your tenants' rent.

COLLECTING RENT VIA MAIL

You may opt to let your tenants sent their rental payment via mail since this choice saves you the time of having to collect their payment personally. However, this method has some issues. For one, the envelope might be postmarked by the required date, yet you could only receive it after several days. Technically, the rent is not considered late, but you will not receive it on time. Another one is when the tenant partially pays their rent. Sending it through the mail will give them some time before you finally find out.

The mail method also gives way to the classic excuse, "Oh, the check got lost in the mail!" Requiring your tenant to a mailing certificate from the postal service for just over a dollar, you can prevent your checks from losing. The certificate serves as proof that your tenant has, indeed, sent the payment. However, the downside here is that it cannot verify the actual amount of money.

ONLINE COLLECTION

Nowadays, online money transfer is a popular option to send funds to almost everyone. Suppose you choose the online method as your primary option for collecting rental payments. In that case, you should also allow other forms of payment (e.g., certified check, cashier's check, and money order) for those tenants who do not have access to online resources).

You can search for reliable rental collection services to find a site that can cater to your needs. Here are some of the best online rent pay services:

- Avail

- PayYourRent

- Cozy

- TenantCloud

- Buildium

Take note that the prices may vary depending on the plan you chose. Some services or plans are basic and straightforward, while others offer other helpful features for a landlord like you. For example, they may include online rent roll, tenant background screening, track maintenance, etc.

You can also collect rent via PayPal and Venmo, which allows instant payment. Venmo, for instance, also enables you to be friends with your tenants on social media. There are some disadvantages to using these platforms. Although PayPal offers free service, it may take the payment transaction several business days to process. They also require the tenant to follow specific instructions to ensure that their payment is not delayed or that you, the recipient of the funds, will not be charged with a fee.

DROP-OFF LOCATION

If you have an office (but not your home office) for your property investing business, you may allow your tenants to drop off their payment at this location. It would be best if you never considered allowing your tenants to drop their payments off at your home address unless, of course, they live at the same address. Instruct your tenant never to drop off envelopes full of cash since somebody can steal them.

Besides, the tenant can also readily claim they left the total amount, but it is a few dollars less.

PAYMENT THROUGH A PROPERTY MANAGEMENT COMPANY

You can choose to outsource rent collection to a third-party property management service provider. Aside from collecting rent on your behalf, they can also handle all maintenance issues, deal with tenant complaints, screen prospective tenants, and look for new tenants. You can sit back and relax; all you need to do is to pay for their services.

PERSONALLY COLLECTING THE RENT

Of course, you can personally collect rental payments if that makes you feel more comfortable. The advantage of this method is that you can immediately have the cash. The downside is that it is time-consuming and quite frustrating when you try to coordinate your pick-up time with your tenants' available time.

GRACE PERIODS AND EXTENSIONS

The usual grace period for rent is 3-5 days, but it varies based on locations, and not all states require landlords or property owners a grace period for rent.

Late fees and grace periods are specified in the lease agreement, and you may charge a certain amount for the late fee along with the number of days after the due date.

Depending on the prevailing law in the area and the terms specified in the lease agreement, a landlord can charge a late fee for rent for each month of delay.

For example, in Washington, the state finds it reasonable for the property owner to charge 20% of the monthly rental or $20, whichever is greater, for late fees,

RAISING THE RENT

https://rentprep.com/property-management/landlords-guide-raising-the-rent/

The easiest and most common way to make rental properties more profitable is to learn how to raise the rent on a tenant. Doing this requires a combination of legal requirements, good business skills, marketing research, and public relations with tenants, making it an essential part of the real estate investment business.

Whether you are a beginner landlord or an expert one who hasn't raised the rent in a few years, the system of raising the rent may look easy but can probably result in loss of both money and tenants if done without too much thinking. So if you are planning to set or raise the rent for your rental property, the tips below will help you get started. Keep in mind that the information here is intended for landlords whose rental properties are not in a rent-controlled zone. Different rules and regulations apply as per state or local government laws.

One of the most frustrating tasks landlords face is how to determine the new rent amount. When they charge too much, they won't be able to either get new tenants or lose their existing ones. On the other hand, they charge too little, and landlords won't generate profit, which is the primary purpose of doing business.

Comparing your rental property to others in your area may be a good starting move but shouldn't be the only factor determining the rent. After all, your rental property is unique.

The additional tips below will also help you get the most accurate idea of rents in your vicinity:

- Compare your rental property to those who look or appear similar to yours. It may include factors like landscaping, amenities like garage or pool, floor area, and more.

- Use rentals that are of the same or close to your rental property's age in years.

- Compare at least five rental amounts that your competitors in the area are charging.

- Look at rental properties that closely match your own rental property's features. It may include the property's number of bedrooms, kitchen or dining area size, etc.

- Find comparisons or competitions to your rental property that best matches your property's style and structure, such as a duplex, bungalow, multi-unit property, or apartment complex.

The ones listed above are crucial rental property factors that online services cannot take into consideration. They won't even pay attention if your bathroom has been remodelled or newly built.

HIRING A RESIDENT MANAGER

Once you get into rental property investing, you have two choices - to manage it yourself or hire a property manager to do the work for you. If you don't have the skill to directly manage your property investment or if the location of your property is far from your residence, you may consider hiring a property manager or a resident manager who is familiar with the business and the local market.

If you choose to hire one, you must consider the value of an experienced and reputable property manager. Property managers aren't cheap, so you need to know the costs and benefits of hiring a property manager.

THE COST OF HIRING A PROPERTY MANAGER

Fees charged by a property manager may vary from one company to another. These depend mainly on the track record - reputation and experience of the management company, the nature of the rental property, the level of services they can provide, and the local market.

For a long-term rental property, they charge as much as 8%-10% of the collected rent.

So if you have a five-unit property that brings in a monthly income of $5,000, it translates to $60,000 a year. $6,000 - which is 10% of your gross income will be for the property manager if you consider hiring one.

THE BENEFIT OF HIRING A PROPERTY MANAGER

Paying 10% of your gross income may seem like a significant expense, but if you consider the benefits it can provide, you will realize it's worth every penny. For one, a property manager has an excellent knowledge of the local rental market ad they have the idea of the rent. If they can successfully rent out your property at a price that is more than you're hoping for, then it can indeed justify the administrative cost.

More than everything, the property manager will be dealing with the daily operations of your business.

- Exhibiting the property to potential tenants

- Verify references provided by tenants

- Conduct credit checks

- Facilitate the move-in process

The property manager will also handle all aspects of marketing related to your property. And because property managers also have other properties available at any given time, they spend more to bring in more tenants.

When a tenant occupies the property, they will be responsible for:

- Collecting the rent

- Dealing with maintenance issues

- Handling tenants complaints and utility bills on your behalf

- Facilitate repairs

- Initiate eviction procedures for non-paying tenants

In general, it can be to your advantage should you hire a property manager. Those who are still starting in their rental property venture will take time to self-manage even just one property. And if you have more than one property to manage, it can be a full-time job as it will take most of your time. Hiring a property manager to take care of the day-to-day operation will allow you more time to oversee other more critical activities. You can focus on your career, family and on expanding your trade while finding the following property for your investment.

However, there are also cases when self-management works to your advantage, like when you want to have first-hand experience on your business, and you treat it like a full-time job. It may be a tedious task, but in the long run, if you have acquired skills and knowledge to master rental property management, aside from bringing the operational cost down, the knowledge you will learn from your experience is worth the time you spent.

WHAT TO DO WHEN TENANTS DO NOT PAY

If a tenant stops paying rent, it is time that you review your lease agreement. Also, check if there is a valid reason for their nonpayment of the rental. In most cases, tenants are just withholding rent because landlords failed to fulfill their part in the lease obligation.

While late payments are often resolved by simply reminding the tenant, you may consider sending the tenant a late rent notice. After doing it, and the tenant still neglects their obligation, consult a local attorney. Your legal attorney may advise you to proceed with the eviction.

HANDLING TENANT MAINTENANCE AND REPAIRS

As a rental property owner, you should get used to hearing and dealing with maintenance issues. It may be by the least a leaky faucet or a very gross, overflowing toilet, but whatever it is, you have to face and deal with these maintenance problems. Moreover, these issues will continue to increase as your tenants or rental properties also increase in number. Some steps are presented here to help you handle tenant maintenance issues though inevitable they may be.

CREATE YOUR MAINTENANCE ISSUES PLAN

First of all, create a basic plan for addressing each maintenance request. It's about how these requests would be submitted and responded to by the person/s in charge. In case you want to have the assistance of a property management company to handle maintenance issues, you will be the one to check if the management company is quick and competent in dealing with all the submitted requests.

RECEIVE YOUR TENANT'S REQUEST

If you prefer to handle the issues yourself rather than having them outsourced, your next step is about your preferred method of receiving a maintenance issue request.

It could be via email, text, phone call, or written notice – whichever you like as long as you address them during regular business hours only to the exemption of emergencies.

CATEGORIZE THE URGENCY OF THE MAINTENANCE ISSUE

Create a list of common issues and categorize them according to their corresponding level of urgency. Categories are high, moderate, and low urgency.

High Urgency – These are issues that need to be fixed or looked upon within the same day or hour.

Moderate Urgency – These are complaints you should deal with within 48 hours.

Low Urgency – These are issues that require fixing within a week.

The following are examples of common issues with their corresponding urgency levels.

Immediate/ High Urgency

- Structural Issues

- Lack of hot water

- Lack of heat in winter

- Majority of the water pipes leak

- Clogged toilet

- Gas leaks or smell

- Lights in common areas or hallways are not functioning.

- Safety issues (e.g., windows or doors that do not lock properly, missing locks)

- Shovelling off snow and putting salt at walkways, stairs, and driveways after snowstorms

Moderate Urgency

- Not working appliances (if supplying the appliances is included in your responsibilities)

- Slow or clogged shower or sink drain

- Interior lights not functioning (if the light fixture is the problem and not just the bulb burning out)

- The air conditioning unit is not working during the summer

- A large hole in the wall

Low Urgency

- Cracked tiles

- Unhazardous flooring damages (e.g., carpet tear, carpet stain, hardwood floor that needs repair or a saddle that comes up)

- Grout coming up

- Running toilet

- Drip or a small leak in the faucet

- Problem on cabinet door hinges

- Problem on interior apartment door hinges

- A door that does not close properly

- Minor hole in the wall

- A draft

- Trim or moulding that needs repair

REPAIRS WHICH AREN'T YOUR RESPONSIBILITY

- Replacing the batteries of your tenant's smoke detector

- Removing trash from the unit

- Damage caused by the tenant or their guests (you could also repair this damage. However, you are allowed to charge a reasonable fee that will cover the cost of materials and contractors/ maintenance personnel fee)

Determine Skill Level Needed for the Maintenance Issue

It would be best if you determined the skill level needed for the maintenance job. Can you attend to it personally, or will you hire someone who is professionally skilled to do the repair? If you think you need professional assistance, call and make an appointment with one.

Gather Materials

If you will be the one to repair the damage, gather the needed materials so you could complete the task.

Notify the Tenant Concerned

If the task is inside the unit, you must call the tenant to schedule the repair. Ask them if it is okay to repair while they are present inside the unit or will they rather have the troubleshooting while they are away.

It also depends on your judgment if the issue needs an immediate response or solution. If you think the repair will require the water, electricity, gas, etc., to be turned off, notify all the tenants in your building before you start the repair.

Have Appropriate Signatures on the Maintenance Request

If you let someone do the maintenance work, be sure to get the handyman's written statement (in specific details) of the work done, the parts needed, and the time it took him to finish the job. Get the repairman and the tenant to sign the statement with the date indicated. You need the tenant's signature for confirmation and if done within the specified time.

Now, if you're the one who repaired, have your tenant sign the maintenance request. The request should have the date, time, and what kind of repair. Were they satisfied with the repair?

BOUNCED RENT CHECKS

To prevent tenants from paying bounced checks or a check without adequate funds, clearly indicate in your rental agreement policies and bounced checks.

As soon as you discover that insufficient funds covered the check paid to you by the tenant, notify them of the issues.

If your lease contract includes a bounced check clause, refer the tenant to it by highlighting that portion so that the tenant is clear of the offence they made.

Regardless of whether the tenant reaches out first to inform you of the issue, don't neglect to send them the official writing. Don't try bending the rules because of compassion, as they can repeat them in the future.

Please keep track of all communications, including times, dates, and topics, to settle in court.

Also, make sure that you have a copy of the bounced check, including notices from the bank informing you of its insufficient funding. Don't forget to let the tenant know the amount of time they need to take action on the issue before you proceed with legal action.

Before taking any legal action on the tenant, check with their bank to see if they have deposited the amount needed to cover the check. Banks sometimes enforce collection, which is why they usually hold the unfunded check, and if a new deposit is made on account of the tenant, that amount will directly be transferred to your account. Check if the issuing bank provides this service.

You may have the option to file either a Notice to Quit or to Pay. It will give the tenant enough time, usually 3-5 working days, to either pay the rent or move out of the property. Some bounce checks exceeding a set amount in dollars may be considered a felony.

What important here is for you to know your rights and always stick to the rules by showing the tenant that you are just and fair. They are more likely to cooperate with you.

WHAT TO DO WHEN A TENANT DIES

Has it ever occurred to you that a tenant may die on the premises of your rental property? What will you do if you face an inevitable situation like that? Sure enough, that is a problem that you would have to deal with if it does happen. Fortunately, issues have solutions. For this situation, there are essential steps that you must follow to secure yourself and your property from legal and financial setbacks.

Although the jurisdictions have nuances depending on the location of your property, you should be knowledgeable and informed about your state and local laws regarding this matter if you have an unfortunate event happening in your rental property.

The following paragraphs would cover the outlined guidelines that you could follow to emerge skillfully and effectively move past this situation: tenant death.

STEPS TO TAKE WHEN A TENANT PASSES

1. Obtain written notice of death

2. Secure your property

3. Coordinate removal of the tenant's belongings

4. Return the security deposit

5. Understand your landlord-tenant laws

6. Get Written Notification

The most significant and initial step you must take when a tenant passes is to get a written death notification. You could get this from the tenant's family member or the tenant's estate executor. Take note that this written notice is essential to begin a legal process of ending the lease, removing your tenant's possession, and getting your property prepared for the next tenant.

In case it is you who discovered your tenant's death, immediately call the police and the emergency contact provided previously provided by the tenant in his application. Secure the property and do not take or remove anything from the area. Wait for the arrival of police authorities and the person listed by the tenant as the one to contact in case of emergency. Then, check what the local and state laws have to say regarding this situation. You must have prepared beforehand in case a situation like this happens.

Secure the Property

When you have received the written notice, secure the property by locking all the windows and doors lest somebody enter the property to steal anything. If the tenant lives in the unit alone, you could change the locks to prevent anyone from entering the unit without you knowing it. You will only be free from the responsibility of securing the tenant's possessions once you handed the keys over to the executor of your tenant's estate or the next kin. If the tenant has no estate executor or next of kin, follow the local and State laws in your area regarding the abandoned property of tenants.

Prepare for the Next Tenancy

Prepare the property for the next tenant by following the given steps:

End the Lease – Though you proceed on lawfully regaining your property, don't forget to be compassionate for the situation of the next of kin or the estate executor. Here are two standard lease options and the right move for each lease:

Month-to-Month Lease – Upon the death of the tenant, they will have a 30-day notice. Notify the executor or tenant's next kin about the expiry date of the lease. Coordinate about removing the deceased tenant's belongings, cleaning, all dues and property transitioning.

Long Term Lease – in this case, the lease does not end automatically upon the tenant's death. It will be passed or transitioned to the executor or next kin. Usually, the executor or next kin would want the lease to end. However, it would help if you worked with them as you complete the lease. Let them know that you will consider the lease a broken agreement and that they (executor/ next kin) are responsible for the entire rent amount until the property has another tenant.

Coordinate Removal of the Tenant's Belongings

You cannot remove your deceased tenant's belongings unless you coordinate its removal with the family or the executor. Set timelines and due dates for the process as you work with them.

If the tenant's lease is a month-to-month lease that will end soon, set timelines that are more appropriate. Typically, it is a two or three-week span for removing the possessions, and then the re-renting process can begin.

But in case of a long-term lease, work with the executor or next kin and establish reasonable timelines. However, they will be required to pay the rent while the transition is still running and while the tenant search is unfinished if it was agreed upon by both parties to treat the death as a broken lease.

But then, if there's no executor or next kin, follow the state and local laws for abandoned tenant property. It may require you to hold the property for a specific period, sell it at auction and then, give back the money to the state.

Return Security Deposit

You can use the security deposit for cleaning fees, unpaid rent, and repairing the damage beyond natural use. Itemize and list all deductions that you made on the security deposit and give that list, with the remaining money, to the estate executor or the next kin. If the fees exceed the deposit, you could petition the tenant's estate or belongings to get the compensation.

Suppose this situation chanced upon you as a landlord of a rental property. In that case, your top priority is to ensure your legal protection by observing the local and state laws regarding a deceased tenant. It will help ease the financial blow you might be getting and simultaneously allow you to find a new renter as soon as possible. If the deceased has the next kin, be compassionate with them and work with them to remove the possessions of your late tenant until the rental is lawfully returned to you again. Once you are ready for the next tenant, be sure that the next one will undergo a thorough tenant screening and rental application.

HANDLING EVICTIONS

One of the toughest challenges you may have to face as a landlord is handling evictions. Nobody wants to deal with evictions because it is simply messy, but sometimes, it is inevitable.

What is an Eviction?

Before we go any further, let us discuss the word "eviction" to ensure that we are on the same page. Eviction is defined as an action of expelling a person, particularly a tenant, from a property. It is a civil process by which a landlord can legally remove a tenant from their rental property.

Eviction may happen when:

- The tenant is often delayed in paying.

- The tenant is not paying rent.

- The tenant and/or their guests did something illegal on the property.

- The tenant and/or their guests caused serious issues, disturbance, or damages for the landlord and/or other tenants.

- The landlord, the landlord's family, the property's buyer, or the buyer's family wants to move in. The landlord's or buyer's family includes their spouse, child, parent, and spouse's parent.

- The landlord wants to demolish the property building, renovate, or use it for something else.

How Eviction Works

It is not uncommon for eviction to happen; it is merely a part of being a landlord and the business of rental properties. When a tenant cannot pay rent or has broken the lease agreement, the landlord can use this as a reason for eviction. Although eviction is something not everybody enjoys, it is something that must be done.

As a landlord, you have to ensure that you understand the proper and legal steps in evicting a tenant.

Understand the Eviction Laws

Eviction laws vary from one region to another. Hence, every landlord must research and understand the eviction laws where they own a rental property. They should consider these laws while drafting lease agreements. On the other hand, it would be wise to hire a lawyer to write the agreement for you.

Provide Reason with Your Tenant

Perhaps you believe that the law may not be on your side, especially when you do not have a legally binding lease agreement with your tenant or you do prefer not to handle an eviction case, try to reason out with your tenant. If you have a cordial relationship with them, it is only decent to ask them to leave the property without going through the eviction case.

This way, they may appreciate your attempt and concede to vacate the property without any further effort.

In case that the reason for eviction is the tenant's inability to pay rent, it is always best to be considerate of your tenant's situation while being firm that they need to be responsible in paying the rent. It is also best to discuss the issue with them in a public location rather than in the rental property itself.

Never take matters into your own hands should the tenant does not concede with your reasoning. Do not put yourself at a disadvantage no matter how frustrated or angry you may feel. The following are some samples of self-help eviction, which are deemed illegal by many jurisdictions:

- Evicting the tenant without going through the legal eviction process

- Removing your tenant's belongings from your rental property

- Locking the tenant out of the rental property

- Shutting off the tenant's utilities, forcing them to leave the property

- Physically coercing the tenant to leave the premises of your rental property

Provide a Formal Eviction Notice

An eviction notice is a formal notice from a landlord to a tenant to vacate a specific rental property. Eviction notices can be the following:

- Notice to Pay or Quit

- Notice to Quit

- Notice of Lease Violation

- Notice of Termination

- Demand for Possession

- Demand for Compliance

Landlords are required to give the tenant a *Notice of Termination* form that clearly states the reason for eviction and when they can begin legal action at the Landlord and Tenant Board. The type of notice form and the duration the landlord must wait upon before applying to the Tenant Board depends on their presented reason for eviction. The Board also provides the notice forms and instruction kits.

In some communities, landlords are required to put an official eviction notice on the property for a particular duration before the tenant can be evicted from the property.

However, in some communities, the landlord must coordinate with the police to post the notice. Alternatively, they must secure a court order before they can evict the tenant.

In general, the notice can be served by delivering it to any adult tenant. It is crucial to determine which rules apply to your given situation. If you are not sure about your obligations, you can always ask a local Landlord or Tenant Advisory Board or an attorney for advice.

File an Application with the Board

After you have given your tenant a notice form and the necessary duration has elapsed, you can proceed to apply to the Board for a hearing date. You must fill out the *Application to Terminate a Tenancy and Evict a Tenant* form and file it at the Board. The Board office clerk will then schedule a date for the hearing and prepare a *Notice of Hearing* form as you wait.

Deliver the Application and Hearing Notice to Your Tenant

Depending on the basis for the application, you are required to furnish a copy of the *Application* and *Notice of Hearing* to your tenant at least five to ten days before the hearing. For instance, if the landlord in Ontario is removing the tenant from his property because the tenant committed an illegal act involving drugs, it is ten days. If the reason is about a disturbance, then it is twenty days.

Apply For a Certificate of Service with the Board OFfice

A landlord must fill out a Certificate of Service form and submit it with the Board to verify that they already delivered the documents. The certificate must be filed no later than five days after the documents were forwarded to their tenant.

Sometimes, a Board mediator may contact both the tenant and the landlord to help them sort out their problems. In the case that the issue is left unresolved through mediation, it will be escalated to a hearing.

Be Prepared and Attend the Hearing

Both the landlord and tenant are required to attend the hearing. A landlord's application may be dismissed if they (or their representative) do not show up. Meanwhile, a Board member may render a decision if the tenant (or their representative) fails to appear.

Eviction Order

If the Board agrees to evict the tenant, an Eviction Order will be issued consequently. The Order will declare when the tenant must vacate the rental property. Suppose that the tenant does not leave by the specified date indicated in the Order, the landlord is instructed to file the Order with the Sheriff's Office so that the sheriff can evict the tenant. Even during such time, a landlord cannot forcibly evict their tenant or change the locks without the sheriff's presence.

Avoiding Future Evictions

Evictions can be a stressful experience. In order to avoid them in the future, you can help yourself by doing thorough research about your potential tenant before stamping your approval in their application. Your research should include performing background checks, confirming employment records, tracking rental history, and checking the prospective tenant's credit.

Even if it is quite an arduous task, make sure to ask their references from past employers to the current ones, as well as their previous landlords or property managers. It would be beneficial to acquire the necessary information from the prospect's former landlords and learn their respective experiences with this tenant. Only after obtaining the needed information should you render the decision. This way, you can spare yourself from future headaches.

CHAPTER 7: DEALING WITH CONTRACTORS

Hiring contractors to work on your property can be costly and stressful. However, knowing how to deal with them will save you unnecessary costs.

A general contractor is a party responsible for overseeing a construction project and entering into a primary contract with the property owner (Viator, 2021). They may assign a subcontractor to do the job or a part of it. Still, the legal responsibility lies on the general contractor being the signatory to the agreement with the property owner.

THE GENERAL CONTRACTOR

When hiring a General Contractor, make sure that you look for a reputable construction company with a proven track record. You can find them online via local directories or through referrals from people you know. Make a shortlist so some background checks by reading online reviews and asking for feedback from people who knew them.

You must have a clear agreement and expectations with them before starting the project. It is essential to maintain clear and good communication with them while allowing them to work on your project. Flexibility and understanding from those involved will help foster a good working relationship that can end up with a better outcome.

SCREENING CONTRACTORS BEFORE HIRING

Meet Potential contractors and start narrowing down your list. Get at least three bids or estimates. Please take note that providing you with an estimate involves time and effort on their part. Therefore, accommodate them as much as possible and notify them immediately once you have chosen someone else.

Avoid "time and material" and "cost-plus" bids.

Once there's no ceiling on how a contractor can spend like in these types of arrangements, you must be nervous.

Low Bidders Won't Save You Money

Often, low bidders are inexperienced, desperate, or cutting corners. While you're thinking, you were able to save money here. Any savings could disappear in many ways.

Check Credentials

Check their license, bond, and insurance.

If things go wrong and not in your favour, the contractor or company should be covered by a company that allows you to file a claim against them. Such claims include:

- Shoddy work

- Failure to complete the job

- Failure to pay for permits

- Theft

- and many more

Liability insurance covers the contractor or company if they damage your property. Workers' compensation insurance is responsible for injured workers, including their medical care and lost wages, regardless of who is at fault. Without these instruments in place, your insurance will take the hit. Therefore, ask for certificates of insurance before contracting them to make sure that policies are active.

THE HANDYMAN

A handyman provides manual work like repairs, plumbing, painting, and other handy jobs around the house. A property manager or landlord needs to know how to hire a handyman because there will always be minor repairs and maintenance needs around your property.

However, before listing the first handyman you can find, there are things that you have to know. Neglecting your due diligence will likely end you up hiring someone that will cause more trouble instead of fixing issues.

Knowing the kind of work you need and how long it will take for the fixing is essential. These will make you decide if you will need an expert for the job or a handyman can handle it. If it involves a minor fix, a handyman can do it, but it makes sense to hire a professional if it is a big issue.

ADVANTAGE OF HIRING A HANDYMAN

- You will need a minimal budget compared to when you hire a specialist or general contractor.

- They are more experienced and therefore can do the job better and fast than you do

- They are often certified for specialized tasks like electrical and plumbing but still affordable compared to someone more technical.

- A handyman can multitask and help you with a lot of work in the maintenance and repair of your property.

DISADVANTAGES

- Hiring a handyman is more expensive than when you do it yourself.

- They are not as experienced as those who are specializing in one particular job.

- They often work alone and do not belong to a team. It means a handyman has limitations in terms of speed, and they had no one to back them up if some issues arise.

Before hiring a handyman, you should have experience with the type of job that you're hiring them to do. Handyman often charges by the hour, so it would be to your disadvantage if you hire someone who has no idea of what he is doing. Besides, amateurs take a longer time to finish the job and often end up with low-quality service. It is why they usually charge you lower, which is why sometimes it is not cost-efficient.

SPECIALISTS

Aside from the general contractor, there are several specialized contractors you can hire, especially when you want to remodel luxury homes or large projects like multi-family high rises. We have here a list of these specialists.

Electrical Specialist

- Electronic control systems

- Electrical works

- Lighting and fire alarm

- Cable splicing

- Communications equipment installation

Plumbing Specialist

- Plumbing repair,

- Piping

- Refrigeration

- Sump pump

- Sewer

Heating and Air-Conditioning Specialist

- Furnace installation and repair

- Heating equipment and boiler installations

- Air conditioning and sir system works

- Gas line hook-up

Plastering Specialist

- Drywall construction and finishing

- Insulation installation

- Acoustical works

- Plaster (plain or ornamental application)

Concrete Specialist

- Sidewalk construction

- Concrete works

- Patio construction

- Stucco works

- Curb constructions

- Blacktop and asphalting

Painting Specialist

- Whitewashing

- House painting

- Wallpaper hanging

- Electrostatic painting

Roofing Specialist

- Roofing repairs and installation

- Roof coating and spraying

- Tinsmithing works

- Skylight installation

- Ceiling installation and repair

- Architectural sheet metal

- Ductworks

- Downspout installation

- Gutter installation

Carpentry Specialist

- Carpentry works

- Framing

- Cabinet works

- Window and door installation

- Joinery

- Trimming and finishing works

Masonry Specialist

- General Masonry

- Concrete block-laying

- Foundations

- Stone setting

- Bricklaying

- Retaining wall constructions

LICENSED VS. UNLICENSED CONTRACTORS

When considering hiring a contractor, you have the option to hire a licensed or unlicensed contractor, each of which comes with its own set of advantages and disadvantages.

A licensed contractor means that they are recognized as legitimate professionals in their industry and not just up for quick grabs of your cash.

A contractor that holds a license for construction work is proven to have met specific standards that the industry requires and maintains those standards when working under a contract agreement. While acquiring a license is not easy or cheap, it also shows that the contractor is committed to their work and abides by their legal commitments to obey laws and regulations on construction.

Having a license is also evidence that the contractor works seriously in every job they are committing to, the fact that an unlicensed contractor can assure you.

While licensed contractors assure you of quality work, unlicensed contractors usually would cut corners to get the job done.

So if you are the property owner who hires an unlicensed contractor – whether they are specializing in a particular job field will have to assume some risks in the quality of work, which might end up with some legal and financial consequences. Suppose the work quality is not up to specific standards required by the local building code, and your contractor did not acquire proper permits. In that case, it could negatively impact your property's value.

Suppose some claims arise due to the poor quality of work done by the unlicensed contractor, you may end up with a void insurance policy or issues with workers' compensation or worker's compensation insurance.

Here are factors that make the difference between a licensed contractor and an unlicensed one.

CHAPTER 8: WRAPPING UP

Rental property can generate income and, with the right strategy, may help build wealth. However, knowledge and interest in this area are crucial to success, just like in any other business. To gain knowledge, you need to spend time and effort. But what is even more important is your interest in knowing the ins and outs of rental property investing.

Without interest, you will not be motivated to learn what you need to learn and may lack the patience to stick to a long-term goal which is a part of an investor's success. You can't just get in into investing and then leave once you get bored or frightened that you will lose everything. Investing is not for those who are weak in heart, for risk is a primary element of investment. Investing takes a longer time to learn, but once you learn the ropes and master its secrets, it is the perfect passive source of income that can bring you great wealth.

If you are still learning, it may be a great idea to partner with someone who got some skills and knowledge in rental property investing. This can mean that if you lack the essential elements needed in running investment – e.g., time, knowledge, and skill, but you have money to fund your project until the end, as long as you have this strong desire to be successful, you can then learn it from someone. This someone could be a trusted seasoned investor who had been there ahead of you and will coach you on rental property investing.

In investing, you can have the option to start on your own and learn from your experience. However, if you can't manage it because of your full-time job and need to hire people to run the business for you, it is still essential to acquire knowledge that will help you control, monitor, gauge, and secure your business. Having a seasoned investor to coach you will provide you with a shortcut to the learning process because they were there ahead of you.

Investing your money in a business and depends blindly on the person you hire can be dangerous, especially when you're new to investing. You may not be the arms and legs of your rental property but ensure that you remain to be its head.

How you see your first deal is very important as it changes the way you see real estate forever. It will test your ability to deal with different situations as well as unleash the inherent skill that you may not even know. You may not be aware that you have the ability to negotiate and persuade the owner of the property you want to buy to sell their property below the asking price. Actively participating in the investment procedure at the start will motivate you to go on and develop momentum once you are successful with your first deal.

While adopting different strategies to investing, remember that the macro approach to investing strategy is very important. You have to see the big picture instead of thinking that everything will be smooth because you're doing well in your local investment. It would be best if you also learn to see the whole industry, its impact, and even the global market situation. Approaching your method from top-to-bottom as in the macro approach means that you have your mindset on long-term investing and not on short-term.

Therefore, if you should invest in rental property investing, consider how appropriate this type of investment will be for you in the long run. Make informed decisions in choosing the best kind of rental property to invest in and not simply because you heard that it's the trend today. What could work for others may not work for you. And because to invest without due diligence, the possibility of losing is stronger.

If you intend to make it big in rental property investing, start with the right mindset, set your goal, make plans, and apply strategies that can help you achieve your goal.

REFERENCES

Banton, C. (2020, September 23). What's the Difference Between ROI and IRR?Retrieved from https://www.investopedia.com/articles/investing/111715/return-investment-roi-vs-internal-rate-return-irr.asp

Ericson, C. (2020, September 18). What Is a Bedroom? Make Sure You Know the Legal Requirements. Retrieved from https://www.realtor.com/advice/sell/what-is-a-bedroom-features/

Frankel, M. C. (2021, April 14). How Much Do I Really Need to Invest in Real Estate? Retrieved from https://www.fool.com/millionacres/real-estate-financing/articles/how-much-do-i-really-need-invest-real-estate/

Hananel, M. (2013, June 13). Capital Reserves for Your Building. Retrieved from http://strategicgrowthre.com/blog/2013/6/13/capital-reserves-for-your-building

Joint Center for Housing Studies of Harvard University. (2017). America's Rental Housing 2017. Retrieved April 9, 2021, from

https://www.jchs.harvard.edu/sites/default/files/harvard_j
chs_americas_rental_housing_2017_0.pdf

Kolomatsky, M. (2017, August 31). Mom and Pop Own Fewer
Rental Units. Retrieved April 9, 2021, from
https://www.nytimes.com/2017/08/31/realestate/institutio
nal-investors-landlord.html

Viator, M. (2021, February 3). General Contractor
Definition: What they Do, and How they Get Paid. Retrieved
from https://www.levelset.com/blog/general-contractor-
definition/

Wikipedia contributors. (2020, May 23). Family (US
Census). Retrieved from
https://en.wikipedia.org/wiki/Family_(US_Census)

www.ingramcontent.com/pod-product-compliance
Lightning Source LLC
Chambersburg PA
CBHW071334210326
41597CB00015B/1453